Testimonials

"Think you don't need a business plan? Think again! Tim Berry brings business planning into the 21st century, marrying the real need for a plan with today's "lean" thinking. The result? Truly the last book on business plans you'll ever need."

> *— Rieva Lesonsky, president/CEO of growbiz media,*
> *author of* Start Your Own Business

"This is by far the best business planning book out there. Every entrepreneur should be forced to read its section on cash flow. It tells you when to stick to the plan and when to change it!"

> *— Barry Moltz, Radio show host, blogger, speaker,*
> *author of* 'Getting Unstuck'

Here it is, folks – from the Galactic Guru of business planning – the way to do business planning in the 21st century. Whether you're a business newbee or an old hand, **Lean Business Planning** takes you by the hand and shows you how to focus your business to be more relevant to the evolving marketplace (customers and employees) and the capital landscape (banks, investors, etc.). No one but Tim Berry could create such a plain language, leading-edge guide. Be smart – listen to Tim.

> *— Jim Blasingame, Author of the award-winning book*
> The Age of the Customer: Prepare for the Moment of Relevance

"Really, really good. I like the fact that you've given a much more tangible business planning tool that gives people a good idea about how to run an **actual** business."

— Vikas Shah, founder of Swisscot Group and Thoughtstrategy.com, President TiE UK North, Visiting Professor with MIT Sloan School of Business

"If you're serious about really running a business, you need this book. It's about getting what you want from your business, getting the right things done, and adjusting quickly to change. Forget the old-fashioned business plan. This is faster, easier, and better. And you'll be grateful for using this proven system."

— Melinda Emerson "SmallBizLady", Bestselling author, Become Your Own Boss in 12 Months, 2nd edition

"In order to thrive today your business must be nimble. Throw out traditional business planning and embrace *Lean Business Planning* and set your business free to dominate."

— John Jantsch, author of Duct Tape Marketing *and* The Referral Engine

"Every business owner should do a lean business plan, and this book shows you how easy it is to do it… and what it will mean to your success."

— Barbara Weltman, author, radio show host, president of Big Ideas for Small Business, Inc.

"Tim Berry wants to change the world, one entrepreneur at a time. And with his help, you can change your world.

"Are you ready to start a business? Thinking about it? Hoping maybe someday to break out of the rat race, become your own boss, and reap the rewards of 'eating what you kill' (as we called in on Wall Street)? This is the book for you.

"**Lean Business Planning** tells you how. Buy this book!

"Traditional business planning works...but you probably don't need a long, detailed planning document to start your business. Newer approaches to strategy cut away the fat, leaving you with a 'lean' approach to planning - and running - your business successfully. Tim, a true "business plan expert" walks you through just the steps you need.

"Follow Tim's advice in **Lean Business Planning** to start and grow your business, you'll be glad you did!"

— *Marc Manley, Director, Small Business Development Center*
at Linn Benton Community College

"Another great book from Tim Berry. Lean business planning is perfect for today's ever-changing small businesses that still need a way to stay on track as they move their chess pieces around the board."

— *The Franchise King®, Joel Libava,*
world's foremost expert on franchise business.

"**Lean Business Planning** is more than a great business book. Tim Berry has created a powerful tool for business owners who are ready to clear away distractions and focus on achieving their goals. Tim's lean planning approach is both accessible and profoundly useful. This book is required reading for every entrepreneur or independent professional who is serious about growing a successful business."

— *Stephen Lahey, Sales and Marketing Consultant*
(StephenLahey.com)

"What stops a lot of small businesses before they even start is the idea of creating a business plan. Although important, it feels like drudge work to them or a ball and chain they'll be tied to forever. They just want to take that idea they're excited about and run with it. That's why the **Lean Business Planning** is so perfect. It provides enough structure to enable a path forward without the perceived constraints of a "formal" plan. Its best feature is the continuous process cycle which is a key strategy small business owners can use to improve the chances for business success. **The Lean Business Planning** allows them to be nimble and quick so they can "work the business," not the plan. This straight forward, step-by-step guide will be helpful for any small business owner to keep handy as they move through their business life cycle."

— Denise O'Berry, author of Small Business Cash Flow: Strategies for Making Your Business a Financial Success

"Forget the old-fashioned business plan. It's not just for startups, or investors; it's to run your business better. Faster, easier, more focused, and quicker to change. Tim Berry's **Lean Business Planning** is a methodology, not just a plan. It's about getting the right things done. A must for every business owner and startup."

— Susan Solivic, THE small business expert, best-selling author, media personality, attorney

"If you think business planning isn't for you, this book will change your mind. Full of actionable tips, examples, and practical advice. Highly recommended."

— Ivan Walsh, entrepreneur

LEAN BUSINESS PLANNING

Get What You Want from Your Business

By Tim Berry

Published by Motivational Press
1777 Aurora Road
Melbourne, Florida, 32935
www.MotivationalPress.com

Manufactured in the United States of America.

ISBN: ISBN: 978-1-62865-213-0

Contents

About the Author

Tim Berry is the best-known and most-respected expert on business planning in the world. Do a Google search for "business plan expert" and you'll find Tim Berry listed first in the organic, unpaid results. Business writers have called him "the business plan guru" and "the Obi-wan Kenobi of business planning," in print, in major media.

Berry founded Palo Alto Software and built it on his own, without outside investment, to multi-million-dollar sales, profits, and cash flow independence. He's a leader in a local group of angel investors. He did business planning for Borland International, a software company that went public in less than four years; for various divisions of Apple Computer for 12 years, and for a collection of clients, large and small for decades. He's the author of *The Plan as You Go Business Plan*, published by Entrepreneur Press, and half a dozen other books published by Entrepreneur, McGraw-Hill, Dow Jones-Irwin, and others. Entrepreneur-celebrity Guy Kawasaki chose to interview Berry as his expert on business planning, and he's been writing on that topic for more than a decade at Entrepreneur, SBA.gov, and other major media.

He has a Stanford MBA degree, an MA in Journalism with honors from the University of Oregon, and a BA *magna cum laude* from the University of Notre Dame.

There's more information about him at timberry.com.

Foreword

Me write a forward for a book on business planning? I recently released version 2.0 of *The Art of the Start*, in which I recommend not writing a business plan.

However, I'm recommending this book because what Tim calls a lean business plan is pretty much what I call the MATT (for milestones, assumptions, tests, and tasks) in *The Art of the Start*.

Tim's lean plan involves bullet points, lists, and tables that help you run your business—as opposed to pitch investors. This includes the metrics you can track, milestones, assumptions, regular review, and frequent revisions.

Use this book to get what you want from your business. Use it to focus, set priorities, follow up on what needs doing, manage people and resources, and get the right things done.

Whether you're looking to start a new business or just run an existing business better, this book will help you set a strategic focus and tactics to match. If you do end up dealing with investors who want a business plan, this book even explains how you can stick with a lean plan and add what investors want.

So I still believe you don't need to write a business plan. However, you do need to set milestones, strategies, tactics, assumptions, forecasts, and budgets. Weave your MATT and get on with your business. That's what this book is about, and that's why I recommend it.

– Guy Kawasaki, Chief evangelist of Canva and author of *The Art of the Start, version 2,0*

Why Lean Planning?

"The plan is useless. But planning is essential."
– Dwight D. Eisenhower

What do you want from your business? Wealth? Fame? Making a better living? Maybe you want more independence. Maybe you want to be able to take time off to coach the kids' soccer. With this book I'm going to help you get what you want. I will show you how focus, priorities, setting expectations and tracking results can help you get what you want from your business. I promise.

Don't sweat the big business plan. Skip the descriptions and explanations. Just do a lean plan. It will help you get where you are going without bogging you down. It's fast, easy, and practical.

Who doesn't like planning a vacation? Decide where you're going to go, look at the activities, attractions, restaurants, hotels, and the route. When I was a kid, we'd get together before our big backpacking trips and plan routes, food, what to pack. As an adult, I'd join my wife planning our family vacations. Planning is part of the fun.

And planning your own business? That too. Set your strategy, and the tactics to execute it. Figure out pricing, marketing, product. It's dreaming and telling stories, and then adding what it takes to make them come true. It's making things happen. It's going from a vague, daunting, hard-to-manage uncertainty to specific educated guesses, linked together, so you can deal with them. Get things done.

Acknowledgements

"Do it. If you fail, we fail together, and we'll manage. We'll take the risk," my wife said, and more than once. So the path to this book depended on my wife saying, "Go for it." And that's not just this book – it's me quitting a good job to go back to school, moving countries, quitting a second good job to go out on my own, me sticking to my software vision, both us risking our house equity and life savings more than once, even though we had kids and just the one income to depend on. So she doesn't get enough credit. She gave me the peace of mind to do my own thing without fear of losing my life relationships over it. And for this book, she helped a lot with the key decisions on size, title, and subtitle.

"It's too big. Cut it back." On the subject of size, that's what I got as feedback from small business expert/authors Barry Moltz and Rieva Lesonsky, and entrepreneur-turned-educator Marc Manly, who read the full first version of this book. "You're trying to do too much," they said. They pointed out the folly of a fat book on lean planning. And I'm grateful.

Several others read pre-release versions and offered suggestions. My thanks here to author-experts John Jantsch, Susan Solovic, Anita Campbell, Joel Libava, Melinda Emerson, Pamela Slim, Barbara Weltman, Stephen Lahey, Denise O'Berry, and Ivan Walsh; and teacher entrepreneurs Vikas Shah, Henry Rock, Gaynelle Jackson, and Tom Burgum.

And Jim Blasingame, the radio talk show host on Small Business Advocate, who shared his advice on publishing, titles, formats, and content.

And special thanks to my daughter Megan, who suggested the subtitle "for a fat business," which still resonates for me. I rejected it, eventually, with help from Rieva, Susan, Barry, and Marc, because these days nobody likes fat. But (damn), I still like that idea.

One-Page Summary

About Lean Planning

Lean business is a better way to do anything in business. Take small steps, look back, track results, see what works, and change often. Lean business planning is a way to optimize your business with focus, specific steps, tracking results, and changing quickly. The principles of lean business planning include do only what you need, track and review often, expect change, develop accountability, and remember it's planning, not accounting.

Do a Lean Business Plan

Section 2, Lean Business Planning Step by Step, is all about how to do a lean business plan. First you define your strategy, such as focus on specific target markets and business offerings to match. Then you set tactics, such as pricing, messaging, and location, to execute strategy. Then you develop concrete specifics, including dates and deadlines. And you also do the essential business numbers, including sales forecast, expense budget, and cash flow.

Then Track, Review, Revise, Manage

The point isn't the plan, but the business you get from it. Do the plan and then adopt an ongoing process of run-review-revise-repeat. When do you revise? When do you stay the course? That's in Section 3, Keeping it Live.

Plus Appendices

A first appendix shows how to calculate <u>starting costs</u>. A second covers <u>sharing your plan</u> with <u>summaries</u>, doing <u>your business pitch</u>, and doing an <u>elevator speech</u>. A third is about <u>planning for angel investment</u>. A fourth is just about LivePlan and doing the <u>lean plan with LivePlan</u>.

Section 1:

Why Lean Business Planning

The goal is getting what you want from your business. Growth, profits, or freedom to set your own schedule? Lean business planning can help. Forget the big business plan, just do a lean plan. It's quick and easy, just a few lists and tables. Then follow it up every month with a quick review. What you'll get from that is an easy way to stay focused, to grow your business, to adjust quickly to change.

Chapter 1

Lean Business

*"**Lean manufacturing**, Lean Enterprise, or **lean production**, often simply, '**lean**,' is a production philosophy that considers the expenditure of resources in any aspect other than the direct creation of value for the end customer to be wasteful, and thus a target for elimination."*

– Wikipedia

In general, lean means strong with muscle but no fat. Lean means useful. No frills. It's not thin, not skinny, just lean.

Lean Manufacturing

The concept *lean manufacturing* started with the Japanese automaker Toyota more than 70 years ago and was adopted by manufacturers worldwide. It focuses only on what adds value. And that avoids waste.

Early on, the lean manufacturing people adopted a

four-step process called PDCA, for plan-do-check-adjust. PDCA came from quality control expert Dr. Edwards Deming. PDCA itself (the idea of the cycle, although the acronym PDCA has various versions) became the gold standard for manufacturing efficiency.

The essential idea is to take small steps, analyze often, and keep watching results and correcting. That's instead of developing big elaborate plans first, then executing in big steps. There's more review, more revision. That's what they call lean.

The benefits are obvious. Consider how the pace of change is constantly increasing. Technology advances faster every year. Adopting a lean process seems like common sense to me.

My business experience has been mainly computers and software, but my formal education was literature first, then journalism, and then business. I learned software by doing. And, I confess, I never had the patience for the big software development plan that some of the larger companies and more schooled developers did. I was the kind of entrepreneur who built the product in a way that got it to market as quickly as possible. There were always new versions to come. I never thought it was finished, and I worked with the next steps and a broad larger vision. I moved in the right direction without taking a long time trying to imagine, in detail, the final product. That was right for me. And it was lean by instinct, before I knew anybody called that lean.

Lean Startups

Eric Ries' book *The Lean Startup* first appeared in 2011 and became the biggest thing in startups in this century.

What is it? It's what the book says, but that's a different book. For the purposes of definition in this book, here's the Wikipedia definition:

> *Similar to the precepts of lean management, Ries' lean startup philosophy seeks to eliminate wasteful practices and increase value producing practices during the product development*

*phase so that startups can have a better chance of success
without requiring large amounts of outside funding, **elaborate
business plans**, or the perfect product.*

– Wikipedia

The emphasis there is mine. Keep this phrase "elaborate business plans" in mind when we move to the next section, on the lean business plan.

First, however, more about lean startups (continuing the Wikipedia text above):

"This is done primarily through two processes, using key performance indicators and a continuous deployment process. Because startups typically cannot afford to have their entire investment depend upon the success of one single product launch, Ries maintains that by releasing a minimum viable product that is not yet finalized, the company can then make use of customer feedback to help further tailor their product to the specific needs of its customers."

– Wikipedia

So the lean startup applies the idea of continuous improvement in steps, or cycles, to starting a new business. The lean startup begins with what they call a minimum viable product, then improves in repetitive cycles, each one involving plan, action, checking results, and revising the plan to start again.

The lean startup idea took off. Experts loved it. Both the lean startup and its suggestion of the minimum viable product now appear nearly everywhere that startups are discussed. There are steadily growing numbers of companion books, follow-up books, conferences, blogs, and lean startup experts and consultants. Few serious attempts at getting new startups funded fail to pay homage to the lean startup and minimum viable product.

Is this a fad? No. I don't think so. This is evolution related to real changes in the business landscape, accelerating technology, and world economies splitting into ever smaller and potentially more efficient pieces. And the fundamental idea is sound: plan more fluidly, take shorter steps, analyze results, and then take more shorter steps. Change is constant, and the pace of change is increasing, so change the way you do business. Make it lean. And that is as true for established businesses as it is for startups.

Chapter 2

Why Lean Business Planning

"However beautiful the strategy,
you should occasionally look at the results."
– Winston Churchill

So we've seen in the previous section that using the term lean in business means focusing on what adds value and avoids waste. It's also about taking small steps and evaluating results often.

Get What You Want from Your Business?

Who cares about planning? Who cares about business plans, lean or otherwise? Planning isn't the point; the point is to get what you want from your business, to work smarter, not harder. It's about better business. Get what you want out of your business.

Stay Focused

Strategy is focus. Don't do everything – you can't – but do the most important things. Don't try to please everybody – you can't – so please the people who matter most, depending on what you want from the business.

Grow Faster

Develop and execute tactics to make strategy real. Make sure what you're doing matches what you think is most important. Figure out optimal pricing, channels marketing, and product (or service) developments.

Adjust Quickly

Make sure you are actually executing your tactics by boiling them down to specific milestones and performance measurements. Track results and compare them to expectations. Develop accountability.

Manage your money. Figure out what you expect to sell, use that to figure out what to spend, and make sure you never run out of cash.

Lean business planning isn't about planning. It's about business. And getting things done. Run your business to make your life better. Don't run your life to make your business better.

It Starts with a Lean Business Plan

Lean business planning adopts the ideas of small steps, constant tracking, and frequent course corrections to planning. It includes only what adds value, without waste. It starts with a core business plan for internal use only, just big enough for optimizing the business. A lean business plan has four essential parts:

1. A strategy summary is a bare-bones description of strategy for management use only.

2. A list of the most important tactics is also bare-bones description, for management use only. It lays out tactics to execute strategy, like pricing, marketing, product or service development, financing, and so forth.

3. Concrete specifics including review schedule, assumptions, milestones, tasks, and performance metrics. Milestones include dates, deadlines, and budgets. Tasks include responsibility assignments and budgets.

4. Essential forecasts including <u>sales</u>, <u>spending</u>, and <u>cash flow</u>. And, if you are starting a new business, also your starting costs.

This lean plan is clearly not the "elaborate business plan" that lean startup experts reject. Unlike the elaborate plan, the lean plan doesn't include carefully worded summaries or detailed business information for outsiders. It is not even a document. It's a collection of lists, tables, and bullet points.

Keep it Live. Use it Well.

Just like lean manufacturing and lean startups, lean business planning is a process of continuous improvement. It takes small steps, analyzes results, and makes corrections. I've revised the classic PDCA cycle to make a lean planning version that I now call PRRR, for plan-run-review-revise.

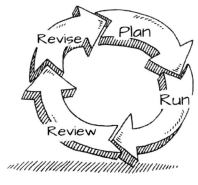

Illustration 2-1: PRRR Cycle

So lean business planning is more than just the lean plan itself. It's the plan plus <u>regular review and revisions</u>. It's never finished. Every latest version will need revision within a few weeks.

Add More Only as Needed

As much as the lean startup experts complain about what they call the elaborate business plan, real businesses, in the real world, do occasionally need to present a business plan to outsiders. They have what I call <u>business plan events</u>, when a business plan is required.

But times have changed. You still don't need the big plan. Do your lean plan and keep it up to date with regular review and revisions. And when somebody asks for a traditional business plan (if they do), then add the extra ingredients you need. That might be a market analysis, maybe an exit strategy, maybe a detailed description of product or marketing plan. Do them as summaries, presentations, or appendices.

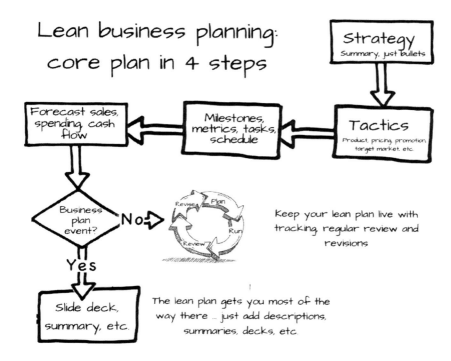

Illustration 2-2: Lean Business Planning

Chapter 3

Principles of Lean Business Planning

"It is not the strongest of the species that survive, not the most intelligent, but the one most responsive to change."

– Charles Darwin

This chapter describes the principles of lean business planning. You might decide, as you read them, that they apply to all good business planning. I believe they do; but that's up to you.

1. Do Only What You'll Use

Lean business means avoiding waste, doing only what has value. Therefore the right form for your business plan is the form that best serves your business purpose. Furthermore, for the vast majority of business owners, the business purpose of planning is getting what you want from the business – setting strategy and tactics, executing, reviewing results, and revising as needed. And that purpose is best served with lean planning that starts with a lean plan and continues with a planning process involving regular review and revision. You keep it lean because that's easier, better, and really all you're going to use.

Consider Illustration 3-1. I put the lean plan at the center because the plan is about what is supposed to happen, when, who does what, how much it costs, and how much money it generates. It's a collection of decisions, lists, and forecasts. It doesn't necessarily exist as a single document somewhere. You use it to track performance against plan, review results, and revise regularly, so the plan is always up to date. I hope it's gathered into a single place, as if it were a document, but it doesn't have to be. And it's only as big as you need for its business function.

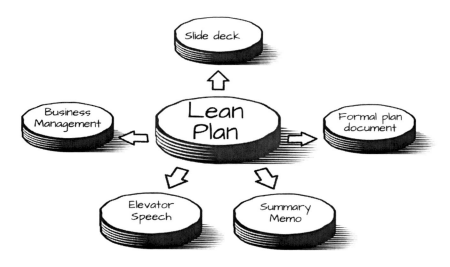

Illustration 3-1: Form Follows Function

Don't confuse the plan with the document, the summary, the slide deck, or elevator speech. The plan is what's going to happen. The other forms are just output.

The main output, and therefore the main purpose, of the lean business plan is better business, which means getting what you want from your business. That's what your lean plan is for and that function determines what's there. Forget the additional descriptions for outsiders until you need them. Wait for that until you have what I call <u>The Business Plan Event</u>. One of the appendices, called <u>Sharing Your Plan</u>, covers how to do summaries, <u>business pitches</u>, and even <u>an elevator speech</u>.

Know Your Market, Yes; Describe, Analyze, Prove – Not Necessarily

You have to know your market extremely well to run your business. Know your market like you know the back of your hand. Know your customers, what they need, what they want, how they find you, what messages work for them, what they read, what they do, and all of that.

What you don't have to do, however, is include any of that in your lean business plan. A lean plan doesn't need rigorous market analysis. It doesn't normally include supporting information — at least, not until later, with the business plan event, when it is actually required.

However, your lean plan is about what's going to happen, what you are going to do. It's about business strategy, specific milestones, dates, deadlines, and forecasts of sales and expenses and so forth. It's not a term paper. Yes, you should know your market. But you don't have to prove it until you're trying to find outside investors.

Form follows function: The function of the lean business plan is getting what you want from your business, not selling something to outsiders.

2. It's a Continuous Process, not Just a Plan

Lean business planning isn't about a plan that you do once. Just like lean manufacturing and lean startups, it's a process of continuous improvement.

With lean planning, your business plan is always a fresh, current version. You never finish a business plan, heave a sigh of relief, and congratulate yourself that you'll never have to do that again. You don't use it once and throw it away. You don't store it in a drawer to gather dust.

However, this kind of regularly updated planning is clearly better for business than a more static elaborate business plan. With lean planning, the plan is smaller and streamlined so you can update it easily and often, at least once a month. Your lean plan is much more useful than a static plan because it is always current, always being tracked and reviewed, frequently revised, and is a valuable tool for managing. You run your business according to priorities. Your tactics match your strategy. Your specific business activities match your tactics. And accountability is part of the process. People on the team are aware of the performance metrics, milestones, and progress or lack of it. Things get done.

Furthermore, even back in the old days of the elaborate business plan, it was always true that a good business plan was never done. I've been pointing that out since the 1980s, in published books, magazine articles, and blog posts. That's not new with lean business planning. It's just more important, and more obvious, than ever before.

So a business plan is not a single thing. It's not something you can buy, or find pre-written. You don't do it and forget it, and you don't find a business plan or have one written for you. If you work with an expert, consultant, coach, or business plan writer, realize that in real use a business plan lasts only a few weeks before it needs to be reviewed and revised. So your value added from the expert has to help you in the long term. If you don't know your plan intimately, then you don't have a plan.

3. It Assumes Constant Change

One of the strongest and most pervasive myths about planning is dead wrong: planning doesn't reduce flexibility. It builds flexibility. Lean business planning manages change. It is not threatened by change.

People say, "Why would I do a business plan? That just locks me in. It's a straitjacket."

And I say: wrong. Never do something just because it's in the plan. There is no merit whatsoever in sticking to a plan just for the plan's sake. You never plan to run yourself into a brick wall over and over.

Instead, understand that the plan relates long term to short term, sales to costs and expenses and cash flow, marketing to sales, and lots of other interdependencies in the business. When things change — and they always do — the plan helps you keep track of what affects what else, so you can adjust accordingly.

So running a business right requires minding the details but also watching the horizon. It's a matter of keeping eyes up, looking at what's happening on the field around you; and eyes down, dealing with the ball – both at the same time.

Change does not undermine planning; actually, planning is the best way to manage change.

Which reminds me that dribbling is one of my favorite analogies for business planning. In soccer or basketball, dribbling means managing the hand-eye or foot-eye coordination of the immediate detail while simultaneously looking up and watching opponents and teammates, and developing plays. When I was coaching kids in soccer, I'd try to help them remember to look up and not just down at the ball. The best players did this naturally.

Here are a couple of additional ways dribbling is like planning:

1. Dribbling is a means to an end—not the goal. Planning is like that too. It's about results, running a business—not at all about the plan itself. Good planning is measured by the decisions it causes. It's about managing, allocating resources, and being accountable. I've written this in several places: "You measure a business plan by the decisions it causes." And this: "Good business planning is nine parts execution for every one part strategy."

2. Think of the moment when the player gets the ball in the wrong end of the court or field. That's either a defensive rebound in basketball, or a missed shot on goal in soccer. The tall player gets the basketball and gives it to the one who normally dribbles up court. Or the goalie gets the ball and gives it to a defender. At that moment, in a well-coached team: 1) there is a plan in place and 2) the player knows the plan but is completely empowered to change it instantly, depending on how the play develops. Business planning done right is very much like that. The existence of a plan—take the ball up the side, pass to the center—helps the team know what ought to happen. But changes—the opponents doing something unexpected—are also foreseen. The game plan doesn't lock the players in to doing the wrong thing or failing to respond to developments. It helps them make instant choices, changing the plan correctly…and when they do, the other players can guess the next step better because of the plan.

4. It Empowers Accountability

It's much easier to be friends with your coworkers than to manage them well. Every small-business owner suffers the problem of management and accountability.

Lean business planning sets clear expectations and then follows up on results. It compares results with expectations. People on a team are held accountable only if management actually does the work of tracking results and communicating them, after the fact, to those responsible.

What gets measured is what gets done

Metrics are part of the problem. As a rule, we don't develop the right metrics for people. Metrics aren't right unless the people responsible understand them and believe in them. Will the measurement scheme show good and bad performances?

Remember, people need metrics. People want metrics. You and your business need metrics.

Then you have to track. That's where the lean business plan creates a management advantage, because tracking and following up is part of its most important pieces. Set the review schedules in advance, make sure you have the right participants for the review, and then do it.

In good teams, the negative feedback is in the metric. Nobody has to scold or lecture, because the team participated in generating the plan and the team reviews it, and good performances make people proud and happy, and bad performances make people embarrassed. It happens automatically. It's part of the planning process. Besides, guilt and fear tactics are the worst kind of fake management.

And you must avoid the crystal ball and chain. Sometimes — actually, often — metrics go sour because assumptions have changed. Unforeseen events happen. You manage these times collaboratively, separating the effort from the results. Your team members see that and they believe in the process, and they'll continue to contribute.

5. It's Planning Not Accounting

One of the most common errors in business planning is confusing planning with accounting. This is true for lean planning too. Your projections, although they look like accounting statements, are just projections. They are always going to be off one way or another, and their purpose isn't guessing the future exactly right, but rather setting down expectations and connecting the links between spending and revenue. Then when you do your monthly reviews, having made the original projection makes adjustments easier.

They are two different dimensions.

Accounting goes from today backwards in time in exact detail. Planning, on the other hand, goes forward into the future in ever-increasing summary and aggregation.

Understanding this difference helps you with the educated guessing involved in making projections. The reports that come out of accounting, called statements, must accurately summarize the actual transactions that happened in the past. For example, a proper and correct Profit and Loss statement in accounting is a report summarizing all the actual transactions recorded as sales, costs, and expenses for a specified period of time (month, quarter, or year).

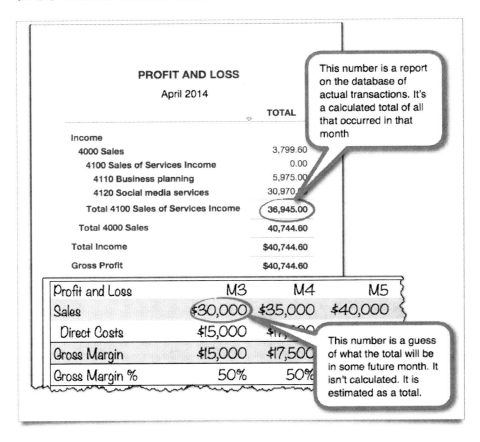

Illustration 3-2: Planning vs. Accounting

But projections, unlike financial statements, are just educated guesses. They aren't reports of a database of actual transactions. Where accounting reports on records in a database, for projections there is no database. We guess what the totals might be.

So you don't try to imagine all the separate transactions in your head, for the future, and then report on them. You estimate the totals. That's not only easier, but better. It's a better match to how the projections help you manage, and how we humans deal with numbers.

Section 2:

Do A Lean Business Plan

Benefits, definitions, and principles aside, this section takes you step-by-step through the process of creating a lean business plan. It's four steps: strategy, tactics, concrete specifics, and essential projections.

Keep it simple. The lean plan is just what you'll use. Yes, you should know your market. Yes, you should have a marketing plan. But almost everything in your lean plan is lists or bullet points, for your own use only.

Chapter 4

Step 1: Set Your Strategy

"The essence of strategy is choosing what not to do."

– Michael Porter

Pull back from the keyboard. Put down that pen. Don't write anything, please, until you've thought through your business' strategy. Start your lean plan with practical strategy.

It's harder to write about strategy than just to do it. They give out PhD degrees for strategy studies, which can be extremely elaborate. People spend entire careers studying strategy as it applies to large corporations.

Strategy is like driving and sex — we all think we're pretty good at it. But simplifying, doing today what will seem obvious tomorrow, is genius. I say the best strategies seem obvious as soon as you understand them. Furthermore, it seems to me that if they don't seem obvious after the fact, they didn't work.

I chose the Michael Porter quote above because I believe it's a great way to see strategy in real world small business and startups. Strategy is what you're not doing. My favorite metaphor is the sculptor with a block of marble — the art is what he chips off the block, not what he leaves in. Michelangelo started with a big chunk of marble and chipped pieces off of it until it was his David. Strategy is focus.

Strategy has to be easy to define. In this chapter I start with my own identity-market-offering (IMO) method, which is pretty simple. But I've also worked in depth, during my consulting years, with several competing strategy frameworks, and every one of them works well if it's applied correctly and executed. In fact, I say you can also define strategy with a story, or a small collection of stories, which I explain in <u>Lead with Stories</u>.

And let's be clear about this: Methods don't matter. Use my IMO method, or use stories, or some other method. What matters is focus, what you do and don't do, and whether it works.

Identity Market Offering (IMO) Method

Think of it as the heart of the business, like the heart of the artichoke: it's a group of three core concepts that can't be separated: Identity, market, and business offering. Don't pull them apart. It's the interrelationship between them that drives your business. Each affects the other two. Illustration 4-1 shows the enmeshed combination.

Illustration 4-1: IMO Strategy Framework

This illustration shows my IMO framework for practical business strategy.

Business Identity

Every business has its core identity. How are you different from others? What are your strengths and weaknesses? What is your core competence? What are your goals? What makes you different?

As an example, imagine the difference between a bicycle retail store owned and operated by a former professional bike racer, and another one owned and operated by a couple with children who like bicycles as a family activity. The first one will probably stock and sell expensive, sophisticated bicycles for the racing enthusiast and extreme long-distance or mountain biking hobbyist. The second will probably emphasize bicycles for children, bike trailers, carriers, and accessories for families.

Notice please how the owners' identity affects strategy in strengths and weaknesses, knowledge and focus, and choice of product and target market.

Part of your identity is what you want from your business. Some businesses are about your lifestyle, or pursuing your passion. Some people want their businesses to grow as big and as fast as they can and are happy to work with investors as owners. Others want to own their own business, even if it has to grow more slowly for lack of working capital. What's your case? If you're committed to a second income in a home office, incorporate that into your identity. Don't look for generalized formulae; let your business be unique. That's differentiation, and it's important.

The Market

Your identity influences your choice of target market. The bike racer focuses on attracting enthusiasts, offering expensive high-end bicycles and equipment. The couple focuses on attracting parents with kids, concentrating on medium-level bikes, trailers, and family-friendly accessories.

Keep your business focused on specific target markets. That bike racer shop owner has to know his products are too expensive for the families, and the families bother the high-end enthusiasts. The family bike shop can't scare away its target market with very expensive racing bikes.

Offering

Your business offering is your product or service. You can already see with the bike shop example how one shop needs one kind of inventory and the other needs a different kind. That's strategy at work. Your identity influences your choice of market, which influences your choice of product. Your choice of product influences your choice of market. They have to work together.

Understand that you can't do everything. The bike shop that caters to families and racers is likely to fail. You can't credibly offer high-end bicycles at bargain prices in a family-friendly atmosphere. If you say you do, nobody believes you anyhow. So you have to focus. Make this focus mesh with your choice of key target customer and your own business identity. All three concepts have to work together.

Seth Godin's book *The Dip* is about being the best at one thing. That's the point of your focus. Since you can't do everything and even if you could, your customers wouldn't believe you, then you need to focus on something that you do well, that people want. Be the cheap and practical bars of soap that sell in volume in the big chain stores, or be a finely-packaged, expensive and sweet-smelling soap that sells in boutiques. Don't try to be both.

Roll Them Up Together

These three things are your business strategy. Don't pull them apart. Don't take them one at a time. Don't ever stop thinking about them. Remember, in planning as well as in all of business, things change. Keep watching for change.

Business Strategy Brainstorming

The following might help you develop your business strategy. These are topics, tools, and suggestions related to identity, market, or offering.

Identity

- Do a SWOT analysis. SWOT stands for Strengths, Weaknesses, Opportunities, and Threats. It's brainstorming, so first list as many points as you can in each category, then pare them down. It's better with a team, but you can do it yourself too.

- Identify your core competence. What do you do better than anybody else? What do you like to do? What are you uniquely qualified to do?

- What makes you different?

- What's special about your brand, your logo, your mission, or your vision?

Market

- Describe your imaginary ideal target buyer. It's like writing about a character in a story. Think of gender, occupation, home, car, favorite media, education, age, and economic situation. Know this person (or, if you are selling to other businesses, do the same for a business).

- Identify your target market as a group of people, kind of buyer, type of company, combination of factors, things people want. It might be "parents of K-6 children," for example. Or small business owners, or knowledge workers, or women over 50.

- Define the problem you solve.

- Who needs your solution to that problem?

- Who isn't in your market? For example, if you are an expensive restaurant with white tablecloths and fine gourmet food, you don't want your market to include families with young children.

- Who doesn't have the problem you solve?

- Who will pay for what you offer?

Business Offering

- What's your solution?

- What are the benefits to the target market?

- What features do you offer?

- What is different about your solution (think about what they call the *secret sauce*)?

- What don't you do that makes you different? (For example, not all restaurants offer takeout food and drive-through.)

- Why is your offering better than others?

- What's your value proposition? (That's the benefit you offer, to what target market, at what relative price. For example, the restaurant offers fine dining for people who appreciate the special occasion, at a price premium.)

Sample IMO Strategy Descriptions

Since this is a first step towards a lean business plan, here's a reminder: The lean business plan is for internal use only. Don't sweat the text. Just do bullets. Here are some examples to help. These are the strategy sections in the lean business plans of a small business social media consultant and a local bicycle retailer. In each case, you can see how the three strategy fundamentals of identity, market, and business offering work together to define a business strategy.

Sample 1: For a small business social media consultant:

This one is actual content from the lean business plan for <u>Have Presence</u>:

Identity

- Familiarity with social media
- Social media for small business
- Understanding of small business and entrepreneurship
- Empathy for small business owners
- Belief in value of small business social media

Market

- Target business owners and entrepreneurs
- They are pressed for time and busy
- They are budget constrained
- They want solutions. Get it done.
- "Don't tell me what to do. Do it for me."

Business Offering

- Do the posting, the actual work; not the strategy
- Maintain thoughtful useful content
- Aim the content at client's potential market
- Offer setup as well as posting

Sample 2: For a bicycle retailer

Identity

- Garrett, the founder, is passionate about bicycling.
- He also has business experience, and capital to invest.
- A team is in place including shop manager, advisor, and investor.

Market

- University town, heavy bicycle use
- Chronic parking problems
- Local community is unusually favorable to bicycling, environmentally friendly, and outdoor activities
- Local bicycle retailers generate complaints. Market seems ripe.
- Frequent refreshing market of students coming in and out
- Families and enthusiasts as well as students

Business Offering

- Spread the offering to include families, commuters, and enthusiasts
- Focused, streamlined high-end offering mainly for visibility
- More breadth of economic options for students and families
- Unbundle service — keep visible prices low, offering service as add-on
- Keep potential of high-end service

Strategy is Focus

There is a very real business use for a strategy summary as part of every business plan, even a lean plan. Since strategy is focus, it leads to some difficult decisions as time goes on. New opportunities arise. Some new opportunities are great additions, offering healthy evolution and growth. Others are dangerous distractions that dilute the business, blur the focus, and bring the business down. The owner, owners, or real core management team have to make these decisions, and they are hard. Normal entrepreneurs want to go into every new market to please everybody they can. So a good strategy summary helps to frame the new opportunities right.

There's no obvious formula for making these decisions. They don't teach it in business school. It's something business owners have to do for themselves. There is always risk and opportunity. So you refer to your strategy summary first, and then think about it.

This should come up in the <u>monthly review sessions</u> I recommend for every lean business planning process for every business. That's in Section 3, Keeping it Live.

Chapter 5

Step 2: Tactics to Execute Strategy

"Strategy without tactics is the slowest route to victory, and tactics without strategy is the noise before defeat."

– Sun Tsu

Lean Business Planning Tactics

Strategy needs tactics for execution. In practical terms, this is your marketing plan, your product or service plan, and other tactical plans.

Aim for strategic alignment: match your tactics to your strategy. You should be able to think of your business as a pyramid, with strategy at the top, tactics in the middle, and concrete specifics at the base, as in Illustration 5-1.

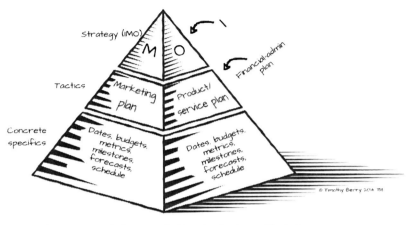

I = identity, M = market, O = product/service (business offering).

Illustration 5-1: IMO Pyramid

Although a book is sequential, your thinking and planning isn't. This chapter is about the middle area of the pyramid, the tactics, mainly marketing and product or service plans. The previous chapter was about the strategy at the top, and the next chapter is about the bottom on the pyramid, the concrete specifics. Don't think of these as separate or sequential. Develop them together. They are sequential here because of format and logistics only.

These tactical plans in your lean plan are as simple as possible, ideally just bullet point references. Don't worry about writing descriptions and explanations, or compiling background information, until you have a real business need to explain them to outsiders. Do worry about thinking all of your marketing and product plans through and planning them well. Even without the big text, you do want to plan and manage your important tactics.

If you're not absolutely sure about your tactics, do your best and remember you're going to review and revise every month from now on.

Marketing Tactics

Marketing, in its essence, is getting your customers to know, like, and trust you. To do that, you must understand your customers: know how and where to find them, how to help them find you, and how to present your business to best match your strategy and business offering. You have to make choices for pricing, messaging, distribution channels, social media, sales activities, and so forth. For your lean plan, these are mainly bullet points. They are defining the tactical decisions that you make. In the lean plan they are for internal use only.

I do recommend, however, that every business leader take a fresh look at the market at least once a year. Markets change, new markets develop, and you don't want to get lost thinking that what was true in the past is still true and will be true in the future.

Product Tactics (or service, or both)

These are about the business offering. Product or service tactics are the decisions you make about pricing, packaging, service specifications, new products or services, product launches, sourcing, manufacturing, software development, technology procurement, trade secrets, bundling, and so forth. Your lean plan contains the decisions you make on these items as bullet points. You know your tactics by heart, so you just list them, briefly, in your lean business plan.

Not sure? Do your best. Only you can decide whether you need to do more testing, research, or prototyping, or launch and develop improvements as you go. That's up to every business owner. There is no certainty ever, so do your best. And remember, you're going to track results, review your metrics, and revise every month. Nothing is written in stone.

Other Tactics

Tactics often include financial tactics, or team building, hiring, recruitment tactics, or logistic tactics related to, say, taking on new office or manufacturing space. I group these in the third part of the pyramid shown in Illustration 5-1.

Overall Strategic Alignment

I like the pyramid metaphor because it highlights strategic alignment from strategy at the top to tactics to concrete specific activities.

Strategic alignment is like silk. It's hard to describe in the abstract, but you know it when you see it. And you know the lack of it when you see that, too.

For example: a local computer systems retailer whose strategy is providing a high level of service to local businesses, offering peace of mind in exchange for prices higher than the box stores, generates strategic alignment by beefing up its service capability with training and additional staff, buying some white vans with messaging about installation and delivery, and dedicating space in the store for a long service counter staffed by technicians in white coats. That same business is out of strategic alignment if it does nothing to improve service, doesn't deliver or install, and hounds customers who are leaving bills unpaid because their equipment wasn't installed correctly and isn't working.

And another example: a restaurant whose strategy is great healthy gourmet meals for special occasions is in alignment when the food, the locale, and the service are excellent; the food sourcing is organic, the cooking is new cuisine, naturally light; and the meals are expensive. A restaurant with that strategy is out of alignment if the food is mediocre, or too heavy on sauces and butter; or the service is poor, or annoying; or it offers drive-through value meals; or it caters to kids under 10.

Business Tactics Checklist

Tactics are easier to recognize than define. Focus on content, what's supposed to happen. Think of tactics as absorbing the traditional marketing plan, product plan, and financing plan. Your next step will be to set these tactics into a plan with concrete milestones, performance metrics, lists of assumptions, and so on.

This brainstorming list should give you an idea of the tactical decisions you make as you execute strategy. In a lean plan, you still want to cover what you need to plan and run your business, but simply jot it down in an organized way, usually bullet points, so you can refer back to it as you flesh out the details. But you don't bother with descriptions.

Marketing Tactics

- Tactics to locate target market, media that work for target market.
- Pricing
- Messaging (tag line, descriptions, etc.)
- Benefits list
- Features lists
- Web presences including web, mobile, social media
- Content marketing
- Advertising
- Packaging
- Channels of distribution
- Margins through channels
- Channel gatekeepers
- Affiliate marketing
- Social media, platforms, metrics, paid posts, etc.
- Events
- Affiliate marketing
- PR (media strategies, interviews, blog posts)

Product Tactics

- Product descriptions and product lists

- Technology, patents, trade secrets, protection
- Price lists, menus, etc.
- Features and benefits lists
- Versions, configurations, new versions, new configurations
- New product (or service)
- Product (or service) updates
- Bundling
- Sources and costs, vendors, suppliers
- Packaging
- Liability problems
- Registration for legal requirements
- Registration in lists of providers

Other Tactics

- Funding needs, raising investment
- Use of funds
- Borrowing, loans, credit lines
- Management team recruitment, compensation
- Benefits

Sample Tactics in a Lean Plan

These are sample marketing tactics for HavePresence.com, the social media service whose strategy was a model for the lean plan strategy section. Notice that the tactics are simple, reminders for management, things to track later with specific dates and deadlines and tracking results. This is from the tactics section of the lean plan.

Marketing and Sales Tactics

- Our location is in the background, the small office location in a residential neighborhood in Eugene, OR. We don't hide the smallness — we show a picture of it on the contact page — but it stays in the background. We could be anywhere, not just Eugene.

- The website is critical location for us, as if it were the store for a retailer. It's our operation center. We need to do continual content, SEO, and updates.

- We use outside experts for SEO and other online marketing. We don't have time for it.

- Pricing: Social media service pricing is all over the map. The current $995 target price is low. We could gradually move that up.

- We should be using chamber of commerce membership for additional marketing/sales in the local area.

- We need to explore email marketing.

Product Tactics

- Manage pricing of social media services.

- Introduce online courses as soon as possible, with connection to WaPow, SchoolKeep, and Udemy

- Complete and market the ebook.

- Develop social media workshop for small business, to be marketed live.

Financial/Admin Tactics

- Use occasional founder inputs to maintain cash flow

- Invest in SEO, content, additional products, at a few hundred per month

- No loans, no investment required beyond occasional founder input

- Stick with the current office

Tactics in a Lean Plan are Simple Lists

You see in these examples that listing tactics in a lean business plan is a long way from the "elaborate business plan" for outsiders. Don't worry about text, editing, and descriptions. Just use bullet points to remind you and your team what the plan is.

Chapter 6

Step 3: Concrete Specifics

"Unless commitment is made, there are only promises and hopes; but no plans."

– Peter F. Drucker

This is my favorite part of a business plan because it's real. It's the specifics you need to track progress, identify problems, and make changes. That includes milestones, measurements, assumptions, and a schedule for regular review and revisions.

Review Schedule

The most important single component of any real business plan – lean plan, traditional plan, or any kind of plan – is a review schedule. This sets the plan into the context of management. It makes it clear to everybody involved (even if that's just you) that the plan is going to be reviewed and revised regularly. All the people charged with executing a business plan have to know when the plan will be reviewed, and by whom. This helps to make it clear that the plan will be a live management tool, not something to be put away on a shelf and forgotten.

For example, in Palo Alto Software, we established the third Thursday of every month as the "plan review meeting" day. In the old days, we brought in lunch and took over the conference room. It wasn't a big deal. We were done in 90 minutes. But we scheduled all the meetings as part of the next year's plan, and key team members knew they should attend, and wanted to be there. Absences happened, but only when they were unavoidable.

If your planning process includes specific responsibilities assigned, managers committed, budgets, dates, and measurability, then the review meetings become easier to manage and attend. The agenda of each meeting should be predetermined by the milestones coming due soon, and milestones recently due. Managers review and discuss plan vs. actual results, explaining and analyzing the differences.

Even if it's just you in your business, you should still do a monthly review. We all benefit from the discipline of a scheduled time to take a step back from the day to day, review progress, analyze results, and make changes. That's called management.

Identify and List Assumptions

Identifying assumptions is extremely important for getting real business benefits from your business planning. Planning is about managing change, and in today's world, change happens very fast. Assumptions solve the dilemma about managing consistency over time, without banging your head against a brick wall.

Assumptions might be different for each company. There is no set list. What's best is to think about those assumptions as you build your twin action plans.

If you can, highlight product-related and marketing-related assumptions. Keep them in separate groups or separate lists.

The key here is to be able to identify and distinguish, later (during your regular reviews and revisions, in Section 3), between changed assumptions and the difference between planned and actual performance. You don't truly build accountability into a planning process until you have a good list of assumptions that might change.

Some of these assumptions go into a table, with numbers, if you want. For example, you might have a table with interest rates if you're paying off debt, or tax rates, and so on.

Many assumptions deserve special attention. Maybe in bullet points. Maybe in slides. Maybe just a simple list. Keep them on top of your mind, where they'll come up quickly at review meetings.

Maybe you're assuming starting dates of one project or another, and these affect other projects. Contingencies pile up. Maybe you're assuming product release, or seeking a liquor license, or finding a location, or winning the dealership, or choosing a partner, or finding the missing link on the team.

Maybe you're assuming some technology coming on line at a certain time. Perhaps you depend on assumptions about market segments, target markets, or which sectors are most important. You're probably assuming some factors in your sales forecast, or your expense budget; if they change, note it, and deal with them as changed assumptions. You may be assuming something about competition. How long do you have before the competition does something unexpected? Do you have that on your assumptions list?

Illustration 6-2 shows the simple assumptions in the bicycle shop sample business plan:

Assumptions

1. Status quo: no major changes in economic picture locally, or beyond local in ways that change the local picture.
2. No significant new competition in the market.
3. No significant market-related events.
4. Significance of social media is growing. We can shift substantial marketing efforts towards social media without suffering loss of branding.
5. Growth of social media means customers control our brand. What's said in social media will be more important than what we say ourselves
6. No significant new developments in technology to change our product portfolio
7. No signicant surprises in fashion to change our product portfolio

Illustration 6-2: Sample List of Assumptions

Milestones

There's no real plan without milestones. Milestones are what you use to manage responsibilities, track results, and review and revise. And without tracking and review, there is no management, and no accountability.

Just as you need tactics to execute strategy, so too you need milestones to execute tactics. Normally you'll look for a close match between tactics and milestones.

Take your milestones list and categorize what's supposed to happen, and when, for ongoing tactics related to products, services, marketing, administration, and finance. They include launch dates, review dates, prototype availabilities, advertising, social media, website development, programs to generate leads and traffic. The milestones set the plan tactics into practical, concrete terms, with real budgets, deadlines, and management responsibilities. They are the building blocks of strategy and tactics. And they are essential to your ongoing plan-vs.-actual management and analysis, which is what turns your planning into management.

Give each milestone at least the following:

- Name
- Date
- Budget
- Person responsible
- Start and end dates
- Expected performance metric
- Relationship with specific tactics and strategy points

You might also have additional information for main milestones. Then make sure all your people know that you will be following the plan, tracking the milestones, and analyzing the plan-vs.-actual results. If you don't follow up, your plan will not be implemented.

You develop your milestones by thinking through strategy, tactics and actions for business offering and marketing. So you can naturally divide them into the same categories as your tactics: marketing and sales, product, and other (where "other" might be, as with tactics, financing activities like raising investment or contracting commercial credit). Or the milestones might be related to legal issues, or managing a team, or logistics like moving or opening a new location.

Illustration 6-3 shows the milestones from the bicycle shop lean business plan:

Milestones Table

Milestone	Due Date	Who's Responsible	Tactics, details
Reconfigure social media accounts	Completed	Terry	Marketing tactics
Investigate Inventory Turns	Completed	Garrett & Leslie	Financial review
Meet with Caroline to review Market Strategy	Completed	Garrett and Terry	
Top 10 customer list	November 13, 2014	Terry	Tactic: focus
Social media program	January 14, 2015	Terry	Let's make sure we're all on the same page with the new year. Social media priorities, content, emphasis, specific plans.
Monthly review	February 19, 2015	Garrett	
Spring promotion plans	March 18, 2015	Terry	Bicycle season coming again. Review general marketing, specific sales and event schedules.
Host bike repair workshop	May 02, 2015	Terry	Tactic: more per customer
Summer marketing programs	May 20, 2015	Terry	Time to establish specific social media content and events for the summer. Participation in community bicycle events.
Summer finance strategy	May 20, 2015	Leslie	Annual financial check-up on cash flow, working capital, and financial needs during the summer slow season.
Review summer inventory plan	June 20, 2015	Garrett	Financial review
Back-to-school programs	August 19, 2015	Garrett	Special sales, promotions, events, and social media spin for the next school year
Annual strategy review session	October 07, 2015	Garrett	SWOT session, strategy and tactics review.

Illustration 6-3: Sample Milestones

Metrics

Developing performance metrics is a critical part of <u>developing accountability</u> as one of the principles of lean planning:

Lean business planning sets clear expectations and then follows up on results. It compares results with expectations. People on a team are held accountable only if management actually does the work of tracking results and communicating them, after the fact, to those responsible.

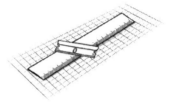

"Metrics" is my favorite word for performance measurements that you track as part of your regular planning process. They are numbers people can see and compare. Make them explicit as part of your lean plan. Show them to the management team as part of the planning and then show the results again and again during your <u>monthly review meeting</u>. Management often boils down to setting clear expectations and then following up on results. Those expectations are the metrics.

The most obvious metrics are in the financial reports: sales, cost of sales, expenses, and so on. Most people in business understand how assigning specific responsibility for those financial numbers, and managing those numbers closely, builds accountability in a business. Those are classic performance metrics.

However, with good lean planning, you can look for metrics throughout the business, aside from what shows up in the financial reports. For example, marketing is traditionally accountable for levels of expenses in the financials, but also generates metrics on websites, social media, emails, conversions, visits, leads, seminars, advertisements, media placements, and so on. Sales is traditionally responsible for the sales reports in the financials, but there are also calls, visits, presentations, proposals, store traffic, price promotions, and so on. Customer service has calls, problems resolved, and other measures. Finance and accounting have metrics including collection days, payment days, and inventory turnover. Business is full of numbers to manage and track performance. When metrics are built into a plan, and shared with the management team, they generate more accountability and more management.

Illustration 6-4 shows simple performance metrics for a bicycle store sample lean plan:

Performance Metrics

Performance Metrics

1. Sales, gross margin, expenses, and cash flow as in the lean plan.
2. Strategic updates 12 per week in Facebook, spaced over all 7 days
3. 32 strategic tweets per week in Twitter, spaced over all 7 days
4. 1 significant planned promotion event per quarter
5. We participate in at least 5 community spirit events per year

Illustration 6-4: Sample Performance Metrics

Developing the metrics required to bring your people into the planning process is very important. Involve the team in deciding what metrics to use. The people in charge often fail to realize how well the players on the team know their specific functions, and how they should be measured.

Of course the starting expectation numbers alone aren't enough. For real accountability, management revisits those numbers regularly, to track progress and make people accountable for results. This is a critical part of planning as steering the business and planning as management.

Chapter 7

Step 4: Essential Business Numbers

"It is far better to foresee even without certainty than not to foresee at all."

– Henri Poincare

How to Forecast Sales

Yes, you can forecast your sales. Don't think you need to have an MBA degree or be a CPA. Don't think it's about sophisticated financial models or spreadsheets. I was a vice president of a market research firm for several years, doing expensive forecasts, and I saw many times that there's nothing better than the educated guess of somebody who knows the business well. All those sophisticated techniques depend on data from the past. And the past, by itself, isn't the best predictor of the future. You are. So let's look at how to forecast sales, step by step.

Your sales forecast won't accurately predict the future. We know that from the start. What you want is to understand the sales drivers and interdependencies, to connect the dots, so that as you review plan vs. actual results every month, you can easily make course corrections. And

If you think sales forecasting is hard, try running a business without a forecast. That's much harder.

your forecasts will become more accurate over time.

Your sales forecast is also the backbone of your business plan. People measure a business and its growth by sales, and your sales forecast sets the standard for expenses, profits and growth. The sales forecast is almost always going to be the first set of numbers you'll track for plan vs. actual use, even if you do no other numbers.

If nothing else, just forecast your sales, track plan vs. actual results, and make corrections; that's already business planning.

Match Your Forecast to Your Accounting

It should be obvious: Make sure the way you organize the sales forecast in rows or items or groups matches the way your accounting (or bookkeeping) tracks them.

Match your chart of accounts, which is what accountants call your list of items that show up in your financial statements.

If the accounting divides sales into *meals, drinks*, and *other*, then the business plan should divide sales into *meals, drinks*, and *other*. So if your chart of accounts divides sales by product or service groups, keep those groups intact in your sales forecast. If bookkeeping tracks sales by product, don't forecast your sales by channel instead.

If you're planning for a startup business, coordinate the bookkeeping categories with the forecasting categories.

Get your last Income Statement (also called Profit & Loss) and keep it in view while you develop your future projections.

- If you don't have more than 20 or so each rows of sales, costs, and expenses, then make the rows in the projected statement match the rows in the accounting.

- If your accounting summarizes categories for you – most systems do – consider using the summary categories in your business plan. Accounting needs detail, while planning needs a summary.

If your categories in the projections don't match the accounting output, you're not going to be able to track plan vs. actual well. It will take retyping and recalculating. And you'll lose the most valuable business benefit of business planning: management, steering your company.

The math is simple

Normally your sales forecast will group sales into a few manageable rows of sales and show projected units, prices, and sales monthly for the next 12 months and annually for the second and third years in the future. Illustration 7-1 shows a quick example from the bicycle retailer named Garrett I've used in other examples (with columns for April-November hidden on purpose, to make viewing easier):

Units	Jan	Feb	Mar	}	Dec	Year1	Year2	Year3
New Bicycles	30	34	36		50	544	600	650
Accessories and Parts	125	142	150		208	2,266	2,400	2,500
Clothing	75	85	90		125	1,360	1,450	1,550
Repair and Service	17	17	17		13	253	300	350
University Patrol Service	5	5	5		5	60	60	60
Total	252	283	298		401	4,483	4,810	5,110

Prices	Jan	Feb	Mar	}	Dec	Year1	Year2	Year3
New Bicycles	$500	$500	$500		$500	$500	$500	$500
Accessories and Parts	$30	$30	$30		$30	$30	$30	$30
Clothing	$60	$60	$60		$60	$60	$60	$60
Repair and Service	$150	$150	$150		$150	$150	$150	$150
University Patrol Service	$100	$100	$100		$100	$100	$100	$100

Sales	Jan	Feb	Mar	}	Dec	Year1	Year2	Year3
New Bicycles	$15,000	$17,000	$18,000	$2	$25,000	$272,000	$300,000	$325,000
Accessories and Parts	$3,750	$4,260	$4,500		$6,240	$67,980	$72,000	$75,000
Clothing	$4,500	$5,100	$5,400		$7,500	$81,600	$87,000	$93,000
Repair and Service	$2,550	$2,550	$2,550		$1,950	$37,950	$45,000	$52,500
University Patrol Service	$500	$500	$500		$500	$6,000	$6,000	$6,000
Total	$26,300	$29,410	$30,950	$3	$41,190	$465,530	$510,000	$551,500

Illustration 7-1: Sample Bicycle Store Sales Forecast

The math for a sales forecast is simple.

1. Multiply units times prices to calculate sales. For example, unit sales of 36 new bicycles in March multiplied by $500 average revenue per bicycle means an estimated $18,000 of sales for new bicycles for that month.

2. Total Unit Sales is the sum of the projected units for each of the five categories of sales.

3. Total Sales is the sum of the projected sales for each of the five categories of sales.

4. Calculate Year 1 totals from the 12 month columns. Units and sales are sums of the 12 columns, and price is the average, calculated by dividing sales by units.

5. The numbers for Year 2 and Year 3 are just single columns; unless you have a special case, projecting monthly results for two and three years hence is overkill. It's a problem of diminishing returns; you don't get enough value to justify the time it takes. Other experts will disagree, by the way; and there may be special cases in which extended monthly projections are worth the effort.

Estimate Direct Costs

A normal sales forecast includes units, price per unit, sales, direct cost per unit, and direct costs. Direct costs are also called COGS, cost of goods sold, and unit costs.

Most people learn COGS in Accounting 101. That stands for Cost of Goods Sold, and applies to businesses that sell goods. COGS for a manufacturer include raw materials and labor costs to manufacture or assemble finished goods. COGS for a bookstore include what the storeowner pays to buy books. COGS for Garrett are what he paid for the bicycles, accessories, and clothing he sold during the month. Direct costs are the same thing for a service business, the direct cost of delivering the service. So, for example, it's the gasoline and maintenance costs of a taxi ride.

Direct costs are specific to the business. The direct costs of a bookstore are its COGS, what it pays to buy books from a distributor. The distributor's direct costs are COGS, what it paid to get the books from the publishers. The direct costs of the book publisher include the cost of printing, binding, shipping, and author royalties. The direct costs of the author are very small, probably just printer paper and photocopying; unless the author is paying an editor, in which case what the editor was paid is part of the author's direct costs.

The costs of manufacturing and assembly labor are always supposed to be included in COGS. And some professional service businesses will include the salaries of their professionals as direct costs. In that case, the accounting firm, law office, or consulting company records the salaries of some of their associates as direct costs.

The Illustration 7-2 shows how Garrett uses estimated margins to project the direct costs for his bicycle store. For the highlighted estimates, the direct entry for bicycles unit cost is the product of multiplying the price by 68 percent. The total direct costs for bicycles in January are the result of multiplying 30 units by $340 per unit.

Units		Jan	Feb	Mar	Apr
New Bicycles		(30)	34	36	40
Accessories and Parts		125	142	150	167
Clothing		75	85	90	100
Repair and Service		17	17	17	23
University Patrol Service Contract		5	5	5	5
Total		252	283	298	335

Prices		Jan	Feb	Mar	Apr
New Bicycles		($500)	$500	$500	$500
Accessories and Parts		$30	$30	$30	$30
Clothing		$60	$60	$60	$60
Repair and Service		$150	$150	$150	$150
University Patrol Service Contract		$100	$100	$100	$100

Unit Costs		Jan	Feb	Mar	Apr
New Bicycles	68%	($340)	$340	$340	$340
Accessories and Parts	50%	$15	$15	$15	$15
Clothing	50%	$30	$30	$30	$30
Repair and Service	20%	$30	$30	$30	$30
University Patrol Service	5%	$5	$5	$5	$5

Direct Costs	Jan	Feb	Mar	Apr
New Bicycles	($10,200)	$11,560	$12,240	$13,600
Accessories and Parts	$1,875	$2,130	$2,250	$2,505
Clothing	$2,250	$2,550	$2,700	$3,000
Repair and Service	$510	$510	$510	$690
University Patrol Service Contract	$25	$25	$25	$25
Total	$14,860	$16,775	$17,725	$19,820

Illustration 7-2: Estimating Direct Costs

Some Quick Notes About Standards

Timing Matters

Standard accounting and financial analysis have rules about sales and direct costs and timing. A sale is when the ownership of the goods changes hands, or the service is performed. That seems simple enough but what happens sometimes is people confuse promises with sales. In the bike store example, if a customer tells Garrett in May that he is definitely going to buy 5 bicycles in July, that transaction should not be part of sales for May. Garrett should put those 5 bicycles into his July forecast and then they will actually be recorded as sales in the bookkeeping actual sales in July when the transaction takes place. In a service business, when a client promises in November to start a monthly service in January, that is not a November sale.

Direct costs also happen when the goods change hands. Technically, according to accounting standards (called *accrual* accounting), when Garrett the bike storeowner buys a bicycle he wants to sell, the money he spent on it remains in inventory until he sells it. It goes from inventory to direct costs for the income statement in the month in which it was sold. If it is never sold, it never affects profit or loss, and remains an asset until some day when the accountants write off old never-sold obsolete inventory, at which time its lowered value becomes an expense. In that case it was never a direct cost.

What's Accrual Accounting and Why You Care

Business accounting is either *cash basis* or *accrual*. I hate how attractive "cash basis" sounds, because accrual is way better, and easier to manage too. Cash basis accounting only works right if you absolutely always pay immediately for every business purchase, and you never buy something before you sell it, and all of your customers pay you in full whenever they buy something from you. So accrual is better.

Here's why, in a few obvious examples.

1. You make a sale when you deliver the goods. If the customer doesn't pay you immediately, in cash basis nothing is recorded. The sale doesn't even show up in your books until the customer pays. In accrual, you record the *accrued* amount as Accounts Receivable, so you keep track of the amount, the date, and the customer who owes it to you. It's obvious that unless you never sell without immediate payment, accrual basis is better.

2. You order some goods. When you receive them, you don't pay for them. You owe the money. You have an invoice to pay. In cash basis, nothing happens until you pay up. In accrual basis, you record the *accrued* amount as Accounts Payable, along with the date, a record of what you bought, and who and when you are supposed to pay. So cash basis is better only if you pay everything immediately; all normal businesses need accrual.

I hate the fact that the accounting standards set a few generations ago chose to call it "cash basis" when you don't record money owed into your books until it's paid; or money you owe until you pay it. It's a terrible idea to keep that information in your head instead of in your bookkeeping. That causes many mistakes as we business owners fail to keep track and remind ourselves of these outstanding obligations. And yet, ironically, they call that "cash basis" accounting. I do wish that the right way to do it, which is accrual accounting, didn't have such an off-putting name.

Gross Margin

Once you have sales forecast and direct costs, you can calculate your estimated gross margin. Gross Margin is sales less direct costs. Gross Margin is a useful basis of comparison between different industries and between companies within the same industry. You can find guidelines and rules of thumb for different industries that give you an industry profile or average gross margin for different industries. For example, industry profiles will tell you that the average gross margin for retail sporting goods is 43%. Every business is different, but knowing the standards and averages gives you some useful comparisons.

The distinction isn't always obvious. For example, manufacturing and assembly labor are supposed to be included in direct costs, but factory workers are paid sometimes when there is no job to work on. And some professional firms put lawyers' accountants' or consultants' salaries into direct costs. These are judgment calls. When I was a young associate in a brand-name management consulting firm, I had to assign all of my 40 hour work week to specific consulting jobs for cost accounting.

Garrett can easily calculate the gross margin he's projecting with his sales forecast. Illustration 7-3 shows his simple calculation of gross margin using the sales in Illustration 7-1 and the direct costs in Illustration 7-2:

	Jan	Feb	Mar
Sales	$26,300	$29,410	$30,950
Direct Costs	$14,860	$16,775	$17,725
Gross Margin	$11,440	$12,635	$13,225
Gross Margin %	43%	43%	43%

Illustration 7-3: Calculating Gross Margin

How do I know what numbers to use?

But how do you know what numbers to put into your sales forecast? The math may be simple, yes, but this is predicting the future; and humans don't do that well. Don't try to guess the future accurately for months in advance. Instead, aim for making clear assumptions and understanding what drives sales, such as web traffic and conversions, in one example, or the direct sales pipeline and leads, in another. And you review results every month, and revise your forecast. Your educated guesses become more accurate over time.

Use experience and past results

- **Experience in the** field is a huge advantage. In the example above, Garrett the bike storeowner has ample experience with past sales. He doesn't know accounting or technical forecasting, but he knows his bicycle store and the bicycle business. He's aware of changes in the market, and his own store's promotions, and other factors that business owners know. He's comfortable making educated guesses. In another example that follows, the café startup entrepreneur makes guesses based on her experience as an employee.

- **Use past results as a guide**. Use results from the recent past if your business has them. Start a forecast by putting last year's numbers into next year's forecast, and then focus on what might be different this year from next. Do you have new opportunities that will make sales grow? New marketing activities, promotions? Then increase the forecast. New competition, and new problems? Nobody wants to forecast decreasing sales, but if that's likely, you need to deal with it by cutting costs or changing your focus.

- **Start with your best guess, and follow up**. Update your forecast each month. Compare the actual results to the forecast. You will get better at forecasting. Your business will teach you.

How to Forecast a New Business or New Product

What? You say you can't forecast because your business or product is new? Join the club. Lots of people start new businesses, or new groups or divisions or products or territories within existing businesses, and can't turn to existing data to forecast the future.

Think of the weather experts doing a 10-day forecast. Of course they don't know the future, but they have some relevant information and they have some experience in the field. They look at weather drivers such as high and low pressure areas, wind directions, cloud formations, storms gathering elsewhere. They consider past experience, so they know how these same factors have generally behaved in the past. And they make educated guesses. When they project a high of 85 and low of 55 tomorrow, those are educated guesses.

You do the same thing with your new business or new product forecast that the experts do with the weather. You can get what data is available on factors that drive your sales, equivalent to air pressure and wind speeds and cloud formations. For example:

- To forecast sales for a new restaurant (there is a detailed example coming in the next section), first draw a map of tables and chairs and then estimate how many meals per mealtime at capacity, and in the beginning. It's not a random number; it's a matter of how many people come in. So a restaurant that seats 36 people at a time might assume it can sell a maximum of 50 lunches when it is absolutely jammed, with some people eating early and some late for their lunch hours. And maybe that's just 20 lunches per day the first month, then 25 the second month, and so on. Apply some reasonable assumption to a month, and you have some idea.

- To forecast sales for a new mobile app, you might get data from the Apple and Android mobile app stores about average downloads for different apps. And a good web search might reveal some anecdotal evidence, blog posts and news stories perhaps, about the ramp-up of existing apps that were successful. Get those numbers and think about how your case might be different. And maybe you drive downloads with a website, so you can predict traffic on your website from past experience and then assume a percentage of web visitors who will download the app (The following sections on Sample Sales Forecast for a Website and Sample Sales Forecast for Email Marketing offer more examples).

So you take the information related to what I'm calling sales drivers, and apply common sense to it, human judgment, and then make your educated guesses. As more information becomes available — like the first month's sales, for example – you add that into the mix, and revise or not, depending on how well it matches your expectations. It's not a one-time forecast that you have to live with as the months go by. It's all part of the lean planning process.

Sales forecast depends on product/service and marketing

Never think of your sales forecast in a vacuum. It flows from the strategic action plans with their assumptions, milestones and metrics. Your marketing milestones affect your sales. Your business offering milestones affect your sales. When you change milestones — and you will, because all business plans change — you should change your sales forecast to match.

Sample Sales Forecast for a Restaurant

Magda is developing a lean plan for a café she wants to open in an office park. She wants a small locale, just six tables of four. She wants to serve coffee and lunches. She hasn't contracted the locale yet, but she has a good idea of where she wants to locate it and what size she wants, so she wants to estimate realistic sales. She assumes a certain size and location and develops a base forecast to get started.

Establishing a base case

She starts with understanding her capacity. She does some simple math. She estimates that with six tables of four people each, she can do only about 24 sit-down lunches in an average day, because lunch is just a single hour. And then she adds to-go lunches, which she estimates will be about double the table lunches, so 48 per day. She estimates lunch beverages as .9 beverages for every lunch at the tables, and only .5 beverages for every to-go lunch. Then she calculates the coffee capacity as a maximum of one customer every two minutes, or 30 customers per hour; and she estimates how she expects the flow during the morning hours, with a maximum 30 coffees during the 8-9 a.m. hour. She also estimates some coffees at lunch, based on 3 coffees for every 10 lunches. You can see the results in Illustration 7-4, as a quick worksheet for calculations.

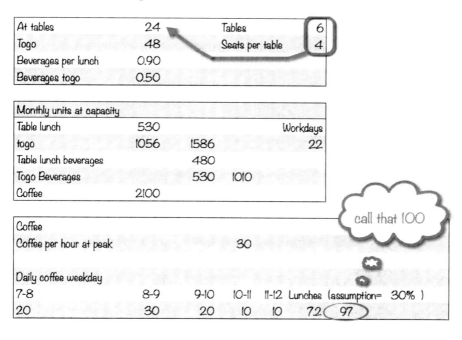

Illustration 7-4: Restaurant Sales Forecast Calculations

Where do those estimates come from? How does Magda know? Ideally, she knows because she has experience. She's familiar with the café business as a former worker, owner, or close connection. Or perhaps she has a partner, spouse, friend, or even a consultant who can make educated guesses. And it helps to break the estimates down into smaller pieces, as you can see Magda has done here.

And, by the way, there is a lesson there about estimating and educated guesses: Magda calculates 97 coffees per day. That's really 100. Always round your educated guesses. Exact numbers give a false sense of certainty.

Café monthly assumptions

She then estimates monthly capacity. You saw in Illustration 7-2 that she estimates 22 workdays per month, and multiplies coffees, lunches, and beverages, to generate the estimated unit numbers for a baseline sample month.

So that means the base case is about 1,500 lunches, about 1,000 beverages, and about 2,000 coffees in a month. Before she takes the next step, Magda adds up some numbers to see whether she should just abandon her idea. At $10 per lunch and $2 per coffee or beverage, that's roughly $15,000 in lunches, $2,000 in lunch beverages, and $4,000 in coffees in a month. She probably calls that $20,000 as a rough estimate of a true full capacity. She could figure on a few thousand in rent, a few thousand in salaries, and then decide that she should continue planning, from the quick view, like it could be a viable business (And that, by the way, in a single paragraph, is a break-even analysis).

From base case to sales forecast

With those rough numbers established as capacity, and some logic for what drives sales, and how the new business might gear up, Magda then does a quick calculation of how she might realistically expect sales to go, compared to capacity, during her first year. That's in Illustration 7-5:

Capacity	Jan	Feb	Mar	Apr	May	June	July	Aug	Sep	Oct	Nov	Dec
Coffee	63%	63%	63%	63%	59%	50%	49%	49%	63%	71%	71%	63%
Lunch	42%	63%	65%	69%	72%	67%	61%	61%	75%	83%	83%	61%
Beverage	46%	69%	72%	76%	79%	74%	67%	67%	82%	91%	91%	67%

Illustration 7-5: Restaurant Monthly Capacity Estimate

Month-by-month estimates for the first year

All of which brings us to a realistic sales forecast for Magda's café in the office park (with some monthly columns removed for visibility's sake). That's in Illustration 7-6:

Units	Jan	Feb	Mar		Dec	Year1	Year2	Year3
Coffee	1,320	1,320	1,320		1,320	15,272	16,000	17,500
Lunches	660	1,000	1,038		960	12,710	14,000	15,000
Beverages	462	697	727		672	8,897	11,000	12,000
Other	100	110	121		235	2,023	2,250	2,500
Total	2,542	3,127	3,206		3,187	38,902	43,250	47,000

Prices	Jan	Feb	Mar		Dec	Year1	Year2	Year3
Coffee	$2.00	$2.00	$2.00		$2.00	$2.00	$2.00	$2.00
Lunches	$10.00	$10.00	$10.00		$10.00	$10.00	$10.00	$10.00
Beverages	$2.00	$2.00	$2.00		$2.00	$2.00	$2.00	$2.00
Other	$5.00	$5.00	$5.00		$5.00	$5.00	$5.00	$5.00

Sales	Jan	Feb	Mar		Dec	Year1	Year2	Year3
Coffee	$2,640	$2,640	$2,640		$2,640	$30,544	$32,000	$35,000
Lunches	$6,600	$10,000	$10,380		$9,600	$127,100	$140,000	$150,000
Beverages	$924	$1,394	$1,454		$1,344	$17,794	$22,000	$24,000
Other	$500	$550	$605		$1,175	$10,115	$11,250	$12,500
Total	$10,664	$14,584	$15,079		$14,759	$185,553	$205,250	$221,500

Illustration 7-6: Restaurant Sample Sales Forecast

Notice that Magda is being realistic. Although her capacity looks like about $20,000 of sales per month, she knows it will take a while to build the customer base and get the business up to that level. She starts out at only about half of what she calculated as full sales; and she gets closer to full sales towards the end of the first year, when her projected sales are more than $19,000.

Important: these are all just rough numbers, for general calculations. There is nothing exact about these estimates. Don't be fooled by how exact they appear.

Notice how she's working with educated guessing. She isn't turning to some magic information source to find out what her sales will be. She doesn't assume there is some magic "right answer." She isn't using quadratic equations and she doesn't need an advanced degree in calculus. She does need to have some sense of what to realistically expect. Ideally she's worked in a restaurant or knows somebody who has, so she has some reasonable information to draw on.

Estimating direct costs

We've seen direct costs already, in the previous section. They are also called COGS, or cost of goods sold, or unit costs. In Magda's case, her direct costs or COGS are what she pays for the coffee beans, beverages, bread, meat, potatoes, and other ingredients in the food she serves.

Just as with the sales categories, forecast your direct costs in categories that match your chart of accounts.

So, with her unit sales estimates already there, Magda needs only add estimated direct costs per unit to finish the forecast. The math is as simple as it was for the sales, multiplying her estimated units times her per-unit direct cost. Then it adds the rows and the columns appropriately. Illustration 7-7 shows the finished example (with some parts cut out for visibility's sake):

Units	Jan	Feb	Mar	Apr	May
Coffee	1,320	1,320	1,320	1,320	1,240
Lunches	660	1,000	1,038	1,100	1,135
Beverages	462	697	727	771	795
Other	100	110	121	133	146
Total	2,542	3,127	3,206	3,324	3,316

Unit Costs	Jan	Feb	Mar	Apr	May
Coffee	$0.40	$0.40	$0.40	$0.40	$0.40
Lunches	$2.00	$2.00	$2.00	$2.00	$2.00
Beverages	$0.40	$0.40	$0.40	$0.40	$0.40
Other	$2.50	$2.50	$2.50	$2.50	$2.50

Direct Costs	Jan	Feb	Mar	Apr	May
Coffee	$528	$528	$528	$528	$496
Lunches	$1,320	$2,000	$2,076	$2,200	$2,270
Beverages	$185	$279	$291	$308	$318
Other	$250	$275	$303	$333	$365
Total	$2,283	$3,082	$3,197	$3,369	$3,449

Illustration 7-7: Sales Forecast with Costs

Here again you see the idea of educated guessing, estimates, and summary. Magda doesn't break down all the possibilities for lunches into details, differentiating the steak sandwich from the veggie sandwich, and everything in between; that level of detail is unmanageable in a forecast. She estimates the overall average direct cost. Coffees cost an average of 40 cents per coffee, and lunches about $5.00. She estimates because she's familiar with the business. And if she weren't familiar with the business, she'd find a partner who is, or do a lot more research.

Sample Sales Forecast for Email Marketing

The idea with forecasting something new is start with something that's easy to guess, then go on from there. That's what Magda does in the example above, going from restaurant layout with chairs and tables, to times of day, and days per week. This next example projects unit sales from email marketing. Here again, the key is to track the assumptions. Illustration 7-8 shows a sample sales forecast for the projected unit sales of the first few months of a product to be marketed via email.

Warning: This is very simplified! May the email marketing experts forgive me for making it look this simple. It isn't; but the basic numbers follow these basic principles.

Email Marketing Assumptions	Jan	Feb	Mar	
Emails sent	20,000	25,000	30,000	40,
Email opens	35%	36%	37%	
Email clicks	8.0%	8.4%	8.8%	
Website views	560	756	982	1,3
Viewed conversion rate	0.5%	0.6%	0.6%	
Unit sales	3	5	6	

Illustration 7-8: Email Sales Forecast Assumptions

1. It starts of course with how many emails get sent. The assumption here is that the marketing department sends out 20,000 emails the first month, 25,000 the next month, and so forth. And let's remem-

ber that while it's easy to type numbers into a spreadsheet, execution requires an effective email message, design and formatting, and a good list of email addresses of real prospects. Targeting is essential.

2. We put assumptions for how many people open the emails into the second row. And the assumption shown for January, by the way, is amazingly high, and quite unrealistic. A business would have to be sending emails to a list of opted-in email addresses for customers or prospects who like this sender a lot. Available information on average emails opened, from MailChimp and other vendors of email services, runs more like 15% to 25%. The numbers here are high.

3. We use the third row for our assumption for how many people click the link on the email. There too, this example is very optimistic. Normal rates rarely get above 2%.

4. Next is website views. With emails sent, emails opened as a percentage, and clicks as a percentage, we can project how many people click an email link and arrive at a website. In January, for example, we take 20000*.35*.08 = 560. Here again, the math is simple. The business behind it -- a good email list, a good email, subject line, text, and links, and offering -- is not simple.

5. Then we project a conversion rate, which is how many people who see the offer on the web choose to buy. The 0.5% (one half of one percent) assumption here is not unusually low. Actual conversion rates depend on how well targeted the people are who arrive at the website, how attractive the offer is, and many other marketing and sales variables.

6. Finally, in the last row, we arrive at projected sales. The indication here is that sending 20,000 emails produces the small unit sales shown here in the bottom row.

From here we would take the unit sales resulting from these assumptions to the main sales forecast, with the structure we use for the sample sales forecast above: units, prices, sales, direct costs per unit, and direct costs.

The spreadsheets would look a lot like the ones for Garrett the bicycle retailer in <u>How to Forecast Sales</u>; and Magda, the restaurant owner, in <u>Sample Sales Forecast for a Restaurant</u>.

Sample Sales Forecast for a Website

The next sample sales forecast shows assumptions for a web business. Here too, we look at the key assumptions that lead to the unit sales forecast. The point is we don't pull a forecast out of thin air, we base it on some sales drivers that we can predict, and, to some extent control -- or at least track and revise. We can look at these in detail in Illustration 7-9.

Web Forecast	Jan	Feb	Mar	Apr
Website organc	200	300	400	500
Website social media	350	500	700	900
Website PPC	2,000	2,000	2,000	2,000
Total website visits	2,550	2,800	3,100	3,400
Website conversion rate	0.5%	0.6%	0.6%	0.6%
Total unit sales	13	17	19	20
PPC Assumptions				
PPC cost per click	$1.00	$1.05	$1.10	$1.15
PPC budget	$2,000	$2,200	$2,400	$2,600

Illustration 7-9: Web Business Sales Forecast

First, estimate the drivers for web traffic

Clearly the web business sales assumptions depend on web traffic. In the first two rows of the forecast, we project reasonable numbers of web visits based on past web experience, search engine optimization (SEO), links that we can predict. In this case we break them into two categories:

1. First, website visits from organic search, based on the site, its contents, the SEO, and so forth. This projection may be optimistic because getting 200 people per month at the outset isn't as easy as writing numbers into a spreadsheet. It takes marketing. Still, it's an assumption we can track.

2. Second, website visits from social media. This assumes active engagement, posts, links, and updates on Facebook, Twitter, and other social media sites.

More about the pay-per-click assumptions

As you can see in the bottom two rows of the forecast, pay per click web traffic depends on two factors: how much you spend on pay-per-click advertising, and how much you pay for each click. A click in this case means somebody who was browsing on some other website, or who did a web search for some specific search word or phrase, clicked a link that went to your website. If you are not familiar with this kind of online marketing, there's a good summary in Wikipedia under "pay per click."

I base my assumptions here on bid-based pay-per-click systems, such as what Google uses. It's like an auction. You bid on what you'll pay when a user who searched for your search term clicks on your link. For example, Illustration 7-10 shows what happened when I searched for the term "restaurant in Eugene OR." Two businesses have paid for the ad placement at the top. One is a restaurant supply business, the other a yellow-pages index. If I clicked on either one, I would go to that website and the business would be charged the pay per click amount. The rest of the search results are Google's favorites, based on Google search algorithms, as the most useful.

Illustration 7-10: Pay Per Click Example

Conversion Rate and Projected Sales

The row in Illustration 7-8 labeled "Website conversion rate" holds the very important assumption for the percentage of website visitors who choose to buy the product. That assumption is half a percent (0.5%) for the first month, increasing to six tenths of a percent (0.6%) in the second month. The total unit sales estimate in "Total unit sales" comes from multiplying the conversion rate in "Website conversion rate" by the estimated web traffic in the row labeled "Total website visits." So, for example, the projected 13 units for January is one half of one percent of the estimated 2,550 web visits.

How to Budget Spending

Along with the revenue forecast, you need to plan and manage spending. Revenue is money coming in, and spending is money going out.

By the way, the word budget, as I use it here, is exactly the same as forecast. The difference between the two is just custom. I could just as easily refer to revenue and spending budgets, or revenue and spending forecasts, as revenue forecast and spending budget. Most people are used to them the way I'm using them, with *forecast* for revenue and *budget* for spending.

There are three common types of spending in a normal business. These are the things you write checks for.

- The first is costs, direct costs, what you spend on what you sell. Those are the costs you have already estimated in your sales forecast.

- The second is your expenses. They are mostly operating expenses, like rent, utilities, advertising, and payroll.

- The third is what you spend to repay debts and purchase assets. I call that "other spending." These are important financial terms that you have to use correctly; so if you have any doubt, investigate what assets are and how debt repayment is different from interest expense, not an expense, but something that absorbs cash and affects the cash available to the business.

Let's look first at the most common kind of spending, the operating expenses.

The Expense Budget

Make sure you understand expenses as a technical financial term. Expenses are spending like payroll and rent that aren't part of direct costs and reduce profits and taxable income. You need to understand that difference if you are going to run a business and manage cash flow. If you have any doubts, please read up on that.

Just as you did for sales forecast and direct costs, try to always project expenses in the same categories you have in your chart of accounts. If your accounting divides marketing expenses into personnel, advertising, and PR, don't project marketing expenses in your business plan as print, online, and social media. This is important

Summary of Operating Expenses

Forecasting your operating expenses is a matter of experience, educated guessing, a bit of research, and common sense. Illustration 7-11 shows a sample expense budget from the same bicycle business plan I used in the Sales Forecast section above (with middle columns cut out):

Operating Expenses	Jan	Feb	Mar	Apr	May	Jun
Payroll	$6,266	$6,966	$7,666	$8,366	$8,367	$8,367
Rent	$2,000	$2,000	$2,000	$2,000	$2,000	$2,000
Marketing	$1,000	$1,000	$2,000	$2,000	$2,000	$2,000
Leased Equipment	$150	$150	$150	$150	$150	$150
Utilities	$125	$125	$125	$125	$125	$125
Insurance	$75	$75	$75	$75	$75	$75
Benefits	$1,567	$1,742	$1,917	$2,092	$2,092	$2,092
Other	$0	$0	$0	$0	$0	$0
Total	$11,183	$12,058	$13,933	$14,808	$14,809	$14,809

Illustration 7-11: Expense Budget for Bicycle Store

All the numbers are educated guesses. Garrett, the bicycle storeowner, knows the business. As he develops his first lean plan, he has a good idea of what he pays for rent, marketing expenses, leased equipment, and so on. And if you don't know these numbers, for your business, find out. If you don't know rents, talk to a broker, see some locations, and estimate what you'll end up paying. Do the same for utilities, insurance, and leased equipment: Make a good list, call people, and take a good educated guess.

Payroll and Payroll Taxes are Operating Expenses

Payroll, or wages and salaries, or compensation, are worth a list of their own. In the case of the bike shop owner, for payroll, he does a separate list so he can keep track. Payroll is a serious fixed cost and an obligation. Garrett's summary budget in Illustration 7-11 has the one line for payroll but it comes from a separate list. He just takes the total into the budget. Illustration 7-12 shows the list:

	Jan	Feb	Mar	Apr	May
Owner	$2,666	$2,666	$2,666	$2,666	$2,667
Asst. Manager	$1,950	$1,950	$1,950	$1,950	$1,950
Asst. Manager	1,650	1,650	1,650	1,650	1,650
Other Employees	$0	$700	$1,400	$2,100	$2,100
Gross salary	6,266	6,966	7,666	8,366	8,367
Benefits %	25%	25%	25%	25%	25%
Benefits	$1,567	$1,742	$1,917	$2,092	$2,092
Total	$7,833	$8,708	$9,583	$10,458	$10,459

Illustration 7-12: Payroll and Payroll Taxes

Notice that the payroll totals from the Personnel Plan show up in the expense budget. And if you look closely (it may take a calculator) at the expense row "Benefits" and compare that amount to the total payroll, you'll see that it's an estimate based on 25 percent of payroll. Garrett uses "Benefits" as a blanket term; it includes what he spends on health insurance and other benefits.

Restaurant Example

Since I've used Magda's new restaurant as an example for the sales forecast, I'm including its operating expenses here too, as a second example.

Simple Operating Expense Budget

Illustration 7-13 shows Magda's lean plan budget for expenses:

Operating Expenses	Jan	Feb	Mar	Apr
Payroll	$8,000	$8,000	$8,000	$8,000
Rent	$1,000	$1,000	$1,000	$1,000
Marketing	$1,000	$264	$244	$224
Leased Equipment	$0	$0	$0	$0
Utilities	$50	$50	$50	$50
Insurance	$50	$50	$50	$50
Payroll Taxes	$1,200	$1,200	$1,200	$1,200
Other	$250	$250	$250	$250
Total Operating Expenses	$11,550	$10,814	$10,794	$10,774

Illustration 7-13: Magda's Expense Budget

And we can also look at Magda's budget for payroll. As with the bicycle store, the operating expenses include the summary of payroll from two rows: Gross Salary is in the row called "Payroll," and Benefits are in the row above titled "Payroll Taxes." Both of these come from the payroll projection in Illustration 7-14:

	Jan	Feb	Mar	A
Owner	$4,000	$4,000	$4,000	$4,00
Managers	$0	$0	$0	
Cooks	$0	$0	$0	
Waitpersons	$3,000	$3,000	$3,000	$3,00
Others	$1,000	$1,000	$1,000	$1,00
Gross salary	8,000	8,000	8,000	8,00
Payroll Taxes %	15%	15%	15%	15
Benefits	$1,200	$1,200	$1,200	$1,20
Total	$1,200	$1,200	$1,200	$1,20

Illustration 7-14: Magda's Budget for Payroll

While Garrett has some other expenses along with payroll taxes in his "Benefits," Magda's bare-bones startup has just the payroll taxes. That's why Garrett's estimate of benefits compared to gross salary is 25%, and Magda's is only 15%. And that's why Magda labels her operating expense row as "Payroll Taxes," while Garrett calls his "Benefits."

Other spending

This is tricky: standard accounting and financial analysis include only sales, costs, and expenses in the calculation of Profit and Loss. However, in the real world, some of what you spend isn't included in either costs or expenses. For example, repaying a loan takes money, but doesn't show up anywhere in the profit and loss. And if you have a product-based business and proper accrual accounting, the money you spend buying inventory doesn't show up in the profit and loss until that inventory sells. Buying a vehicle or production equipment isn't tax deductible and isn't an expense; but it costs money. The rule of thumb is that all expenses are tax deductible, but not all spending is an expense.

What to do? Plan and track your operating expenses for sure. And if you need to handle loan repayments, purchasing assets, distributing profits, owners' draw, or other spending outside of profit and loss, keep those in your spending budget. Keep track of them. Plan for them.

Understand Starting Costs

Startup costs are a special case that applies to startup businesses only. They are the sum of the assets you need to purchase before you start, plus the expenses you incur before you start. My advice on how to estimate starting costs is waiting for you later, in <u>Appendix A</u>.

Beware of Cash Flow Traps

Let me show you the difference between profits and cash with a simple example. Take the estimates we have in the previous sections for the sales, direct costs, and operating expenses of Garrett's bicycle shop. Put them together and you have Illustration 7-15 as projected operating income (remember that income and profit are the same thing):

	Jan	Feb	Mar	Apr	May	Jun
Sales	$26,300	$29,410	$30,950	$34,960	$43,290	$38,040
Direct costs	$14,860	$16,775	$17,725	$19,820	$24,705	$21,720
Operating expenses	$11,183	$12,058	$13,433	$14,808	$14,809	$14,809
Operating Income	$258	$578	-$208	$333	$3,776	$1,511
Cumulative Profit	$258	$835	$628	$960	$4,736	$6,248

Illustration 7-15: Sample Projected Profit

Now we compare that to a simple cash flow projection based on the assumption that the store makes 90% of its sales on account (to be paid later) and its customers wait two months to pay those invoices. (That would be unusual for a bicycle store, yes, but it's the common case for most existing business-to-business companies.) Also, let's assume Garrett keeps about a month's worth of sales as products in the store, called inventory, that customers can buy; and he has to buy those products in advance of selling them. The result is cash flow vastly different from profits, as you can see in Illustration 7-16:

Money Received	Jan	Feb	Mar	Apr	May	Jun
Cash Sales	$2,630	$2,941	$3,095	$3,496	$4,329	$3,804
Payments Received	$0	$0	$23,670	$26,469	$27,855	$31,464
Total Received	$2,630	$2,941	$26,765	$29,965	$32,184	$35,268
Money Spent	Jan	Feb	Mar	Apr	May	Jun
Operating Expenses	$11,183	$12,058	$13,433	$14,808	$14,809	$14,809
Purchase Inventory	$30,000	$19,000	$19,000	$22,000	$30,000	$18,000
Total Spent	$41,183	$31,058	$32,433	$36,808	$44,809	$32,809
Cash Flow	-$38,553	-$28,117	-$5,668	-$6,843	-$12,625	$2,459
Cash Balance	-$38,553	-$66,669	-$72,337	-$79,179	-$91,804	-$89,345

Illustration 7-16: Sample Projected Cash Flow

Conclusion: the difference between profits and cash, in this case, is more than $90,000 for a business selling about $30,000 monthly. That business would be profitable but bankrupt for lack of cash. And the change in the two scenarios is just cash flow, not a penny of sales, cost of sales, or expenses. No prices are changed, no new employees added, and no changes made in salary.

Illustration 7-17 shows you how that difference looks graphically:

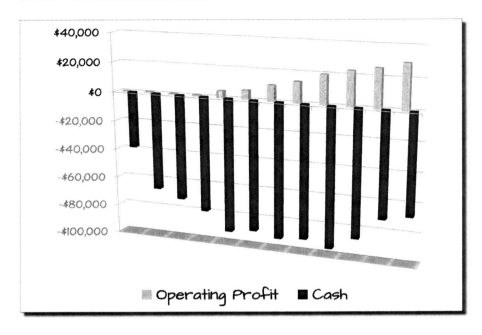

Illustration 7-17: Cash Balance vs. Operating Profits

Assess Your Cash Flow Risk

Your business might not have the factors that make cash flow so different from profits. Maybe managing sales and expenses is enough for your business. Illustration 7-18 shows you how to tell whether or not you need to calculate cash flow:

1.)	Product Inventory	Give yourself 1 point if you deal with product inventory you have to buy and pay for before you can sell it. Add another point for each month of average inventory.	
2.)	Sales on Credit (or on account; as in most business-to-business sales)	1 point if you have to wait for customers to pay invoices (instead of collecting all in cash, check or credit card when you make the sale or deliver the service). Add an additional point for every month beyond one that you wait, on average, for customers to pay.	
3.)	Deposits in Advance	If you added a point for 2.) above, subtract 1/2 point for having customers pay significant (35% or more) deposits up front.	
4.)	Other Spending	Add another 1 point if you have to pay significant principle payments on debts, or purchase significant assets (equipment, vehicles, etc.)	
5.)	Accounts Payable	Subtract 1/2 point if you pay expenses by collecting invoices from vendors and waiting a month or more before paying	
	Now add up your score.	If your total score is more than 1, you should do real cash flow, linked to projected Profit and Loss and Balance Sheet, as in Chapter 19, *Projecting Cash Flow*	

Illustration 7-18: Assess Your Cash Flow Risk

If you scored less than one, heave a sigh of relief and watch your sales, cost of sales, and expenses very carefully. You don't have to calculate cash flow as a separate exercise. Develop and manage projections of sales, cost of sales, operating expenses, and other spending including repayment of debt and purchase of assets. Put your sales, costs, expenses, and other spending into a worksheet showing your projections for the next 12 months. And maybe, just to be sure, you continue reading with the next section on Cash Traps, and the one after that, showing a cash example.

If you scored 1 or more, you might still read the next two sections just to be sure, but face it, you can't afford not to manage cash flow carefully. Aside from just lean business planning, you need to fully understand and manage cash flow; or have somebody on your team who does.

What to Watch

True cash-only businesses are extremely rare. Such a business would have to sell entirely in cash, check, or credit card; not ever have to buy inventory or anything else before it makes a sale, and would immediately pay for everything it buys. Maybe that's a crafts-market artisan? A writer? I'm not sure; but that's why I put the <u>cash flow risk assessment</u> ahead of this section. When in doubt, plan for the worst. I am sure that most of us, as business owners, have to deal with the more common problems of cash flow.

Important: In projections and business planning, cash means liquidity, like checking account balance and liquid securities, not coins and bills.

Profits aren't cash.

Profits aren't cash; they're accounting. And accounting is a lot more creative than you think. You can't pay bills with profits. Actually, profits can lull you to sleep. If you pay your bills and your customers don't, it's suddenly business hell. You can make profits without making any money. Profits are an accounting concept; cash is what we spend. We pay the bills and payroll with cash. While a lean business plan doesn't necessarily include a full-blown financial forecast (at least not until the business plan event, when it will be needed), of course it should include planning for cash.

This should be a pretty simple concept, but it becomes difficult because we're trained to think about profits more than cash. It's the general way of the world. When people do the mythical business plan on a napkin, they think about what it costs to build something, and how much more they can sell it for, which means profits.

However, you can be profitable without having any money in the bank. And what's worse is that it tends to happen a lot when you're growing, which turns good news into bad news and catches people unprepared.

Cash Flow Isn't Intuitive.

Don't try to do it in your head unless you have that extremely simple business. Making the sale doesn't necessarily mean you have the money for it. Incurring the expense doesn't necessarily mean you paid for it already. Inventory is usually bought and paid for and then stored until it becomes cost of sales. Being profitable doesn't guarantee you have money in the bank. Most of us have to take the extra step to plan cash, not just profits.

Growth Sucks Up Cash.

It's paradoxical. The best of times can be hiding the worst of times. One of the toughest years my company had was when we doubled sales and almost went broke. We were building things two months in advance and getting the money from sales six months later. Add growth to that and it can be like a Trojan horse, hiding a problem inside a solution. Yes, of course you want to grow, but be careful because growth costs cash. It's a matter of working capital. The faster you grow, the more financing you need.

What's Receivables? When you make a sale, but the client or the customer doesn't pay you immediately, you record the amount they owe you as Accounts Receivable.

Every Dollar of Receivables is A Dollar Less Cash.

Although it's not intuitive, it's true that more receivables mean less cash. You can do the analysis pretty quickly. Assets have to equal capital minus liabilities, so if you have a dollar of receivables as an asset, that pretty much means you have one dollar less in cash. If your customers had paid you, it would be money, not accounts receivable.

This comes up all the time in business-to-business sales. In most of the world, when a business delivers goods or services to another business, instead of getting the money for the sale right away, there is an invoice and the business customer pays later. That's not always true, but it is the rule, not the exception. We call that "sales on credit," by the way, and it has nothing to do with sales paid for by credit card (which, ironically, is usually the same as cash less a couple of days and a couple of percentage points as fees). Some people call it "sales on account."

We can use this in making financial projections: the more assets you have in receivables, the less in cash.

Example: A company running smoothly with an average of a 45-day wait for its receivables has a steady cash flow with a minimum balance of just a little less than $500,000. The same company is more than half a million dollars in deficit when the number of its average collection days goes to 90 instead of 45. That's a swing of more than a million dollars between the two assumptions. And that's in a company with less than $10 million annual sales, and fewer than 50 employees. And the company in the sample case that preceded this section, with sales of about $30,000 a month, has a gap between operating profits and cash flow of more than $90,000. You can click here to jump back to those numbers and a chart to go with it.

And the trick is that profit and loss doesn't care about receivables. You have as much profit when you sell $1,000 that your customers haven't paid yet as when you sell $1,000 that your customers paid instantly in cash. Obviously, the cash flow implications are different in either case.

Every Dollar Spent on Inventory is a Dollar Less Cash.

When your business has to buy stuff before it can sell it, that's called inventory. It's one of your assets. And keeping a lot of inventory can do bad things to your cash flow, unless you don't pay for it.

This can be pretty simple math. If having nothing in inventory leaves you with $20,000 in cash, then having $19,000 in inventory leaves you with only $1,000 in cash. That is, if you've paid for the inventory. That's because your other assets, your liabilities, and your capital are all the same.

Sometimes, of course, you cannot pay for that inventory, which means you have more payables, and your cash balance is supported by those payables. That's my next point…

Every Dollar of Payables is a Dollar More of Cash.

While receivables and inventory suck up money by dedicating assets to things that might have been cash but aren't, paying your own bills late is a standard way to protect your cash flow. The same basic math applies, so if you leave your money in cash instead of using it to pay your bills, you have more cash.

It's called "accounts payable," meaning money that you owe. Every dollar in accounts payable is a dollar you have in cash that won't be there if you pay that bill. The same problem you have when you sell to businesses is an advantage you have when you are a business. The seller's accounts receivable is the buyer's accounts payable.

Now I don't want to imply that you don't pay your bills, or that it doesn't matter. Your business will have credit problems and a bad reputation if it doesn't pay bills on time, or if it is chronically late with payments. Still, a lot of businesses use accounts payable to help finance themselves.

Working Capital is a Survival Skill.

Technically, *working capital* is an accounting term for what's left over when you subtract current liabilities from current assets. Practically, it's money in the bank that you use to pay your running costs and expenses and buy inventory while waiting to get paid by your business customers.

Bankers Hate Surprises.

Plan ahead. You get no extra points for spontaneity when dealing with banks. If you see a growth spurt coming, a new product opportunity or a problem with customers paying, the sooner you get to the bank armed with charts and a realistic plan, the better off you'll be.

Watch The Vital Metrics.

If you have sales on credit, *Collection days* measure how long you wait to get paid. If you manage physical products, *Inventory turnover* is a measure of how long your inventory sits on your working capital and clogs your cash flow. And for any business that takes advantage of the standard commercial credit, *Payment days* measure how long you wait to pay your vendors. Always monitor these three vital signs of cash flow. Estimate them 12 months ahead and compare your plan with what actually happens.

Managing Cash Flow

At this point you've done your sales forecast and spending budget. Unless your business is extremely simple, you should still plan for cash. You already did most of the projections.

To really project cash flow properly you need to understand the relationship between the three main accounting statements, which are beyond the scope of lean business planning. I do recommend that every business owner should plan cash flow using correct financial calculations that link the main financial statements to make a connected system in which every change affects the whole system, and the balance always balances. However, for the purpose of your lean plan, you may choose to manage cash flow by watching the flow of sales and expenses and key balances.

Section 3:

Keeping it Live: Continuous Process

Lean business planning is a continuous process. The first lean business plan is just the first step. For the rest of your business' life, you review the plan once a month. Compare actual results to what you had planned, determine what steps to take to optimize, and revise the plan.

You'll find that this helps in many ways:

- Maintain focus
- Align the team with priorities
- Address changes in the marketplace as they happen
- Tune strategy and tactics to what's working and what's not working

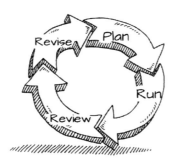

Chapter 8

The Monthly Review Session

"It is a bad plan that admits of no modification."

– Publilius Syrus

S cheduling the monthly review was the first of the concrete specifics of your plan. I suggested a set schedule such as the third Thursday of every month, so you can set the meeting into your calendar ahead of time. Make sure you get that meeting onto the schedules of every person on the team who should attend. Make sure it's a relatively short but also extremely useful meeting.

Expect resistance when you introduce good planning process into an existing organization. I have several decades of first-hand experience with this. It takes leadership. Some people mistrust planning process because they fear you will use accountability – tracking performance metrics and results – against them. Others mistrust it because of the myth that having a plan means you have to follow it, no matter what.

Take the review session schedule very seriously. You're the leader. You set priorities. You give it importance. You can use the review schedule to set meetings months in advance, so team members can plan around it and be present. And make sure you're present too. If you don't show up, or if you allow others to miss it, then it's not that important.

The need for leadership is especially important in the beginning. After you have years of history with monthly review sessions, then maybe you can miss an occasional session and trust your team to do it well. But the early meetings are essential.

Standard Meeting Agenda

Review sessions become second nature in time, but as you start with your planning process, the more detail in the agenda, the better. Here are some things to include.

Review Assumptions

Start every review session with your list of assumptions. That's why you list them in the plan. Assumptions change often. You don't build a plan on a set of assumptions and then forget about them, because they are probably changing. So once a month you review assumptions.

Assumptions lead to a key decision. You always deal with the question of when to revise the plan and when to stick to it. If assumptions have changed, then the plan should change. If not, then you look further. Maybe you need to stay the course and maybe not.

Review Milestones

You can set some of the main agenda points of the review sessions in advance. Your plan includes milestones, that is, dates and deadlines. Use them to set review session agendas. For example, if your plan includes a milestone for product launch in September, then even in January (several months ahead), you can add that item to the August, September, and October review sessions. In August you check the last details, in September you go over the launch as it's happening, and in October you review the results and execution.

Review Performance Against Planned Metrics

Reap the benefits of good planning and accountability. Use the review session to share performance metrics, track results, and identify problems, opportunities, and threats. Let there be some peer pressure as key managers share their results.

The most obvious and standard review is the plan vs. actual analysis of financial results. In accounting and finance, the difference between the plan and actual results is called *variance*, and the exploring it is called *variance analysis*. This is a very important monthly process. Look at key financial metrics including sales, sales by product or line, direct costs, expenses, profits, balance sheet including assets and liabilities, and of course the cash balance and cash flow.

Remember that performance metrics, accountability, and peer pressure require leadership. You want this to be about good decisions, productivity, and collaboration, not threats or fear. Make sure your managers feel safe bringing up expectations and revising metrics. Encourage them to evaluate metrics often and to bring up problems with metrics ahead of time, not after the fact.

Good planning encourages collaboration. Managers should know that it's better to bring problems up ahead of time than hide them until after the fact. If the various factors that influence total sales show problems over the summer, you want to know about it, and deal with it promptly. You don't want to wait until results are bad in October, and then react in November. Instead, in good planning process, managers bring up problems before they happen. Problems are discussed, solutions put in place where possible, and expectations revised. You want to know ahead of time if sales are going to slip, so you can adjust expenses accordingly. That happens in an atmosphere of collaboration, not criticism.

That collaboration should extend to other metrics, beyond just the financials. For example, suppose a plan includes leads generated through an online webinar program. It's set to generate 500 new leads in October.

However, the marketing team learns in July that some unforeseen development – not something the team could control – will really hurt the attendance of the October webinar, and decrease the expected leads. With good planning process, the problem comes up in the July or August plan review session. The team adjusts both performance metrics and related marketing activities ahead of time. What you don't want, of course, is the problem being hidden or avoided with no actions taken, and then performance metrics are disappointing for October.

Leadership sets the tone. Problems are supposed to come up. Good management wants to get bad news fast. And collaboration is the rule.

Gathering the Team

Make sure your review sessions include the right people.

Even if it's just you, a one-person company, you should still do your monthly review sessions. Plan ahead and take the time to actually step away from the daily routine and review your plan, assumptions, and results. And revise your plan as needed.

In a business, the review session should include everybody in the company who has responsibility for executing the plan. Use your judgment. In a startup with just a few people, review sessions might include the whole team. By the time you have 20 people, review sessions probably include five or six. Being at the review session should be both an obligation and a privilege. Don't include so many people that your meeting is unmanageable. Match your organization structure and your culture.

Plan vs. Actual Analysis

Look at a simple example of how plan vs. actual analysis works. Where do these numbers come from, and what do they mean? And, further on, how do you use them to manage better?

Here's some simple vocabulary: In accounting and financial analysis, the difference between plan and actual is called *variance*. It's a good word to know. Furthermore, you can have positive (good) or negative (bad) variance.

Positive Variance:

- *It comes out as a positive number.*
- *If you sell more than planned, that's good. If profits are higher than planned, that's good too. So for sales and profits, variance is actual results less planned results (subtract plan from actual).*
- *For costs and expenses, spending less than planned is good, so positive variance means the actual amount is less than the planned amount. To calculate, subtract actual costs (or expenses) from planned costs.*

Negative Variance:

- *The opposite. When sales or profits are less than planned, that's bad. You calculate variance on sales and profits by subtracting plan from actual.*
- *When costs or expenses are more than planned, that's also bad. Once again, you subtract actual results from the planned results.*

Sales Variance Example

I'd like to show you this with a simple example. Let's start with a beginning sales plan, then look at variance, and explore what it means. In Illustration 8-1 you see sales, actual, and variance for bicycle unit sales for the month of March. You can see in this illustration that the plan was for 36, actual sales were 31, so the variance was -5. The plan for April was 40 units, actual sales were 42, so that's a positive variance of 2.

Plan

Units	Mar	Apr
New B...	36	40
Accessories and Parts	150	167
Clothing		
Repair		
Universi		
Total		
Prices		
New Bi		
Access		
Clothing		
Repair		
Universi		
Sales		
New Bi		
Access		
Clothing		
Repair		
Universi		
Total		

Actual

Units	Mar	Apr	May
New Bicycles	31	42	47
Accessories and Parts	175	171	210
Clothing	164	121	212
Repair	23	25	27
University Patrol Service Contract	5	5	5
Total	398	364	501

Prices	Mar	Apr	May
New Bicycles	$615	$421	$604
Accessories and Parts	$23	$23	$36
Clothing	$49	$47	$37
Repair and Service	$145	$142	$152
University Patrol Service Contract	$95	$95	$95

Sales	Mar	Apr	May
New Bicycles	$19,053	$17,682	$28,388
Accessories and Parts	$4,017	$3,933	$7,560
Clothing	$8,104	$5,687	$7,844
Repair and Service	$3,345	$3,550	$4,104
University Patrol Service Contract	$475	$475	$475
Total	$34,994	$31,327	$48,371

Variance

Units	Mar	Apr	May
New...	-5	2	-3
Accessories and Parts	25	4	2
	74	21	87
	6	2	0
Contract	0	0	0
	94	27	86

	Mar	Apr	May
	$115	-$79	$104
	-$7	-$7	$6
	-$11	-$13	-$23
	-$5	-$8	$2
Contract	-$5	-$5	-$5

	Mar	Apr	May
	$1,053	-$2,318	$3,388
	-$483	-$1,077	$1,320
	$2,704	-$313	$344
	$795	$100	$54
Contract	-$25	-$25	-$25
	$4,044	-$3,633	$5,081

Illustration 8-1: Plan vs. Actual Sales

Units

Regarding units, in March the store sold five fewer bicycles than planned; and in April, it sold two more than planned. That's a negative variance for March and positive for April. But wait – there's more.

Prices

I use prices in this example to point out that plan vs. actual analysis offers a lot of good information. Look at the prices of bicycles for March, April, and May. You can see there was a price promotion going on in April, right? The price of bicycles went down. It was supposed to be $500 on average, but it ended up as $79 less than that. And the increased units over plan were not enough to compensate for the lower average price per unit. The value of April sales of bicycles ended up $2,318 less than planned. The store's total sales for the month suffered, and ended up $3,633 less than planned.

Management

This simple example shows why regular review and managing plan vs. actual results is steering the company, and management. The variance analysis in this case leads to insight about price promotions. It might generate discussions about what went wrong. It might change some future decisions about price promotions. And of course it needs to generate some spending adjustments to compensate for the less-than-expected sales. The team has to work together, not looking to assign blame, but rather to gain insight and to adjust the business.

Expense Variance Example

Illustration 8-2 shows the expense variance for the same period, for the same bicycle store:

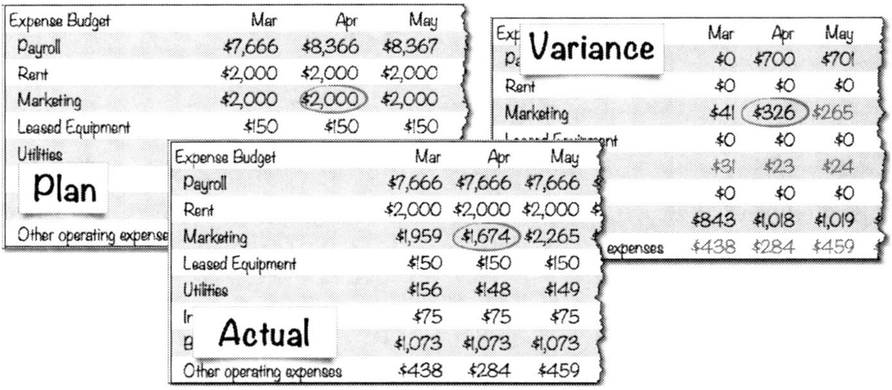

Illustration 8-2: Plan vs. Actual Expenses

In this case, you can see that the actual marketing expenses were $326 less than planned, which is a positive variance, because an expense less than planned is a positive variance by definition. But is this good?

Analyzing the Marketing Expense Case

Here again, I want to show you the management implications of plan vs. actual. With the sales plan vs. actual we saw a sales promotion based on price. Apparently it failed, because the price attracted too few buyers to compensate the store for the discount.

But was the price the problem, or did somebody fail to execute on marketing? Is spending less than planned, during a promotion, a good thing? The prices came down but maybe the marketing department failed to tell people about it. Where is the management problem? What needs to be corrected? These are examples of good questions coming from plan vs. actual analysis.

Furthermore, let's revisit the results with a look at what happened in May. In that month, the marketing expense was higher than planned, by $326. That's a negative variance, an expense higher than planned. But another thing that happened in May – you can see it in the sales variance – was a price boost back to above plan, and sales revenue well above plan. So maybe that negative variance was actually good marketing, well executed.

So if you and I are running the bicycle store, we need more information. We need to look at results and talk about them with the team, to take advantage of what's working, and correct what isn't. And the variance analysis – plan vs. actual – provides the clues. Then it requires management to follow up and take action.

The Management in Plan Vs. Actual

What's important is not the accounting, the calculations, but rather the resulting management. Garrett, the bike storeowner, watches the variance every month. He looks for indications of problems, or unexpected positives, so he can react. In this picture, the variance is negligible. The forecast was remarkably close to actual results. Still, Garrett should investigate why he's selling fewer accessories and parts than planned, and whether the up and down of repair and service is worth reviewing.

The point is the management. Lean business planning is about the management, not the hard numbers. What should be done, given the variance, to make the company better?

Chapter 9

Planning as Management

"It is better to take many small steps in the right direction than to make a great leap forward only to stumble backward."

– Chinese proverb

The workable lean business plan is the first step in a planning process that will help you steer your business and optimize your management to get what you want your business to do for you. Follow up with the review schedule, review plan vs. actual results every month, and keep your plan alive and growing. Keep it lean, keep it live.

Repeat this step monthly for the rest of your business life. A going business is always revising its plan. Change is constant. Follow your review schedule monthly. A real business plan is never done. If your plan is done, your business is done.

Experts know that <u>planning is to manage change</u> and is not voided by change. As your business evolves, so will your business plan. You'll add pieces to fit the needs. You'll need to add product and marketing information to coordinate development, deployment, messaging and timing. You'll have to add to your financials to account for loans and capital equipment, which become part of a balance sheet.

The normal lean planning process is what I call the PRRR cycle, for "plan, run, review, and revise." This is my lean-planning version of the traditional lean business technique that started with lean manufacturing and also includes the lean startup.

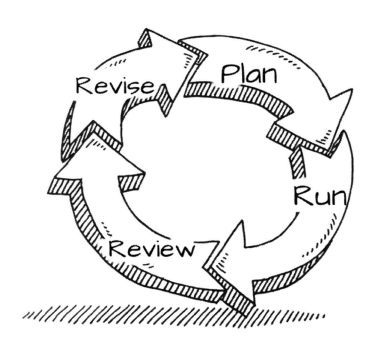

Management and Accountability

Every small-business owner suffers the problem of management and accountability. It's much easier to be friends with the people you work with than to manage them well.

Correct management means setting expectations well and then following up on results. Compare results with expectations. People on a team are held accountable only if management actually does the work of tracking results and communicating results, after the fact, to the people responsible.

Metrics are part of the problem. As a rule we don't develop the right metrics for people. Metrics aren't right unless the people responsible understand them and believe in them. Will the measurement scheme show good performances and bad performances?

The metrics should be built into the plan. Remember, people need metrics. People want metrics.

Then you have to track. That's where the lean business plan creates a management advantage, because tracking and following up is part of its most important pieces. Set the review schedules in advance, make sure you have the right participants for the review, and then do it.

In good teams, the negative feedback is in the metric. Nobody has to scold or lecture, because the team participated in generating the plan and the team reviews it, and good performances make people proud and happy, and bad performances make people embarrassed. It happens automatically. It's part of the planning process.

Emphasize collaboration and cooperation. Sometimes -- actually, often -- metrics go sour because assumptions have changed. Unforeseen events happened. You manage these times collaboratively, separating the effort from the results. People on your team see that and they believe in the process, and they'll continue to contribute.

Stick to the Plan or Change It?

As you work with lean planning, when you get to reviewing and revising, these questions will come up:

These are valid questions. And there are no easy answers. You won't find some set of best practices to make this easy. You'll end up deciding on a case-by-case basis.

Do I stick to the plan, or change it? If I change it, then is my plan vs. actual valid? Doesn't it take consistent execution to make strategy work?

The Arguments for Staying the Course

In one of my earlier books on business planning, I wrote this about consistency and planning:

It's better to have a mediocre strategy consistently applied over three or more years than a series of brilliant strategies, each applied for six months or so.

This is frustrating, because people get bored with consistency, and almost always the people running a strategy are bored with it long before the market understands it.

I was consulting with Apple Computer during the 1980s when the Macintosh platform became the foundation for what we now call "desktop publishing." We take it for granted today, but back in 1985 when the first laser printers came out, it was like magic. Suddenly a single person in a home office could produce documents that looked professional.

What I saw in Apple at that time was smart young managers getting bored with desktop publishing long before the market even understood what it was. They started looking at multimedia instead. They were attracted to new technologies and innovation. As a result, they lost the concentration on desktop publishing, and lost a lot of market potential as Windows vendors moved in with competitive products.

That argues for staying the course. Strategy takes time.

The Arguments for Revising the Plan

On the other hand, there is no virtue in sticking to the plan for its own stake. Nobody wants the futility of trying to implement a flawed plan.

You've probably dealt with the problem of people doing something "because that's the plan" when in fact it just isn't working. I certainly have. That kind of thinking is one reason why some Web companies survived the first dotcom boom and others didn't. It also explains why some business experts question the value of the business plan. That's sloppy thinking, in my opinion: confusing the value of the planning with the mistake of implementing a plan without change or review, just because it's the plan.

How to Decide: Stay the Course or Revise the Plan

This consistency vs. revision dilemma is one of the best and most obvious reasons for having people — owners and managers — run the business planning, rather than algorithms or artificial intelligence. It takes people to deal with this critical judgment.

One good way to deal with it is by focusing on the assumptions. Identify the key assumptions and whether or not they've changed. When assumptions have changed, there is no virtue whatsoever in sticking to the plan you built on top of them. Use your common sense. Were you wrong about the whole thing, or just about timing? Has something else happened, like market problems or disruptive technology, or competition, to change your basic assumptions?

Do not revise your plan glibly. Remember that some of the best strategies take longer to implement. Remember also that you're living with it every day; it is naturally going to seem old to you, and boring, long before the target audience gets it.

A Good Business Plan is Never Done

This is true for all business planning, not just lean business planning:

A good business plan is never done. If your business plan is finished, then your company is also finished.

It's a lot like the legendary farmer's axe, that has had its handle changed four times and its blade changed three times, but it's still the same axe.

As your company gets used to the planning process, the business plan is always a work in progress. It gets a big refreshment every year, and a review and course correction every month.

While this is true for all business planning, the lean plan is especially good for dealing with this essential reality, because the lean plan is faster and easier to do and therefore easier to review and revise. It's streamlined, just big enough to run the business.

The idea is that you always have your lean plan up to date. You meet every month to review it. Every so often, as business plan events come up, you spin out of your business plan a formal output piece, whether it's a pitch presentation, an elevator speech, or a full-fledged elaborate business plan document.

Do understand, always, that the document, summary, or pitch is not the plan; that's just output from the plan. It's the latest version. But the lean business plan goes on, like steering, walking, dribbling, and navigation.

Don't ever wait for a plan to be done. Get going.

Business Plans are Always Wrong, But Vital

It is a simple statement: all business plans are wrong, but nonetheless vital.

It is paradoxical, perhaps, but still very true.

All business plans are wrong because we're human, we can't help it, we're predicting the future, and we're going to guess wrong.

But they are also vital to running a business because they help us track changes in assumptions and unexpected results in the context of the long-term goals of the company, long-term strategy, accountability, and, well, just about everything lean planning represents.

Appendices

This section contains more detailed information, tips and traps, suggestions, food for thought, and more discussion. Chapter by chapter, I left the additional information contained here for this last section because people are different: some want all the detail in order, and others want to go quickly through the main points.

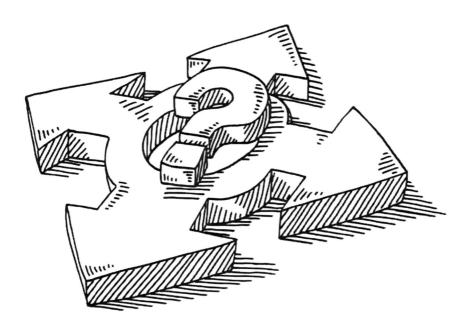

Appendix A

Starting Costs

"I knew that if I failed I wouldn't regret that,
but I knew the one thing I might regret is not trying."
— Jeff Bezos

Knowing the starting costs before you start a business is a matter of two simple lists:

- **Startup expenses**: These are expenses that happen before the beginning of the plan, before the first month of operations. For example, many new companies incur expenses for legal work, logo design, brochures, site selection and improvements, and signage. If there is a business location, then normally the startup pays rent for a month or more before opening. And if employees start receiving compensation before the opening, then those expenses are also startup expenses.

- **Startup assets**: Typical startup assets are cash (in the form of the money in the bank when the company starts), business or plant equipment, office furniture, vehicles, and starting inventory for stores or manufacturers.

Timing and Startup Costs

Startup costs happen before launch. On the first day of business, the launch, a normal business startup has already incurred its startup expenses and has acquired its startup assets. It has figured out financing, including borrowing what it needs to borrow, establishing initial investment, and setting up an initial balance that saves the startup expenses as a loss at startup (which will be deductible against profits later on, to reduce taxes).

Startup costs often include rent and payroll that are paid before launch. The difference between these as startup expenses and these as running expenses is timing, and nothing else. The same is true of starting inventory; it's a startup cost because it's needed before the launch, or at the time of the launch. Otherwise it's the same as inventory purchased during the regular course of business.

A Simple Starting Costs Example

Illustration A-1 shows an example of projected starting costs for the bicycle store I use in this book as an example. Notice how Garrett estimates his starting expenses and starting assets required, and also estimates his funding including liabilities and capital.

There are some basic accounting principles involved. Notice how the total $124,650 startup costs on the left are balanced by $124,650 startup funding on the left. That's because accounting (double entry bookkeeping too) requires matching money spent to money raised. Otherwise, the balance wouldn't balance.

Startup Expenses		Startup Funding	
Legal	$1,600	Liabilities	
Logo etc.	$50	Accounts Payable (Outstanding Bills)	$17,650
Promotional Materials	$100	Notes Payable	$2,000
Contractors	$800	Other Current	$10,000
Insurance	$150	Long-term Liabilities	$70,000
Computer	$200	Total Liabilities	$99,650
Other	$250	Capital	
Total Startup Expenses	$3,150	Owner	$25,000
		Investors	$0
Startup Assets		Total Capital	$25,000
Cash Required	$35,000	Total Startup Funding	$124,650
Startup Inventory	$17,000		
Other Current Assets	$8,000		
Long-term Assets	$61,500		
Total Assets	$121,500		
Total Requirements	$124,650		

Illustration A-1: Starting Costs for Bicycle Store

Notice that on the same worksheet Garrett used to estimate starting costs, he also estimated starting funding, on the right side of the illustration. Books have to balance, so the initial estimates need to include not just the money you spend, but also where it comes from. In the case above, Garrett had to find $124,500, and you can see that he financed it with Accounts Payable, debt, and investment in various categories.

Another Simple Starting Costs Example

Illustration A-2 offers another simple example: the starting costs worksheet that Magda developed for the restaurant I used in Chapter 7 for basic numbers. Magda's list includes rent and payroll, the same as in her monthly spending, but here they are included in starting costs because these expenses happen before the launch.

Startup Expenses		Startup Funding	
Legal	$1,000	Liabilities	
Logo etc.	$200	Accounts Payable (Outstanding Bills)	$12,000
Rent	$2,000	Notes Payable	$8,000
Payroll	$1,500	Other Current	$0
Insurance	$150	Long-term Liabilities	$20,000
Computer	$400	Total Liabilities	$40,000
Other	$750	Capital	
Total Startup Expenses	$6,000	Owner	$20,000
		Investors	$0
Startup Assets		Total Capital	$20,000
Cash Required	$12,000	Total Startup Funding	$60,000
Startup Inventory	$3,000		
Other Current Assets	$3,000		
Long-term Assets	$36,000		
Total Assets	$54,000		
Total Requirements	$60,000		

Illustration A-2: Restaurant Sample Case Starting Costs

I included rent and payroll because they point out the importance in timing. The difference between these as startup expenses and running expenses is timing, and nothing else. Magda could have chosen to plan startup expenses as a running worksheet on expenses, starting a few months before launch, as in the illustration below. I prefer the separate lists, because I like the way the two lists create an estimate of starting costs. But that's an option.

How to Estimate Starting Costs

Obviously the goal with starting costs isn't just to track them, but to estimate them ahead of time so you have a better idea, before you start a new business, of what the financial costs might be. Breaking the items down into a practical list makes the educated guess a lot easier. Ideally, you know the business you want to start, you are already familiar with the industry, so you can do a useful estimate for most of the startup costs from your own experience. If you don't have enough firsthand knowledge, then you should be talking to people who do. For others, such as insurance, legal costs, or graphic design for logos, call some providers or brokers, and talk to partners; educate those guesses.

Starting Cash is the Hardest and Most Important

How much cash do you need in the bank, as you launch? That's usually the toughest starting cost question. It's also prone to misinformation, such as those alleged rules of thumb you can find everywhere, saying you need to have a year's worth of expenses, or six months' worth, before you start. It's not that simple. For most businesses, the startup cash isn't a matter of what's ideal, or what some expert says is the rule of thumb – it's how much money you have, can get, and are willing to risk.

The best way is to subtract spending from sales for your monthly budget, which shows how much (at least in theory, according to assumptions) the startup really needs in cash to support the business as it grows, before it reaches a monthly cash flow break-even point. Magda did that to determine the $12,000 needed as starting cash for her restaurant. Note how, in Illustration A-3, the lowest point in cash is slightly less than $12,000:

Money Received	Jan	Feb	Mar	Apr	May	Jun	Jul	Aug	Sep	Oct	Nov	Dec
Cash Sales	$9,598	$3,126	$3,571	$4,262	$4,535	$3,532	$2,500	$2,668	$5,458	$7,211	$7,256	$3,283
Payments Received	$0	$0	$1,066	$1,458	$1,508	$1,585	$1,615	$1,504	$1,389	$1,408	$1,718	$1,912
New Loans	$0	$0	$0	$0	$0	$0	$0	$0	$0	$0	$0	$0
New Investment	$0	$0	$0	$0	$0	$0	$0	$0	$0	$0	$0	$0
Total Received	$9,598	$3,126	$4,638	$5,721	$6,043	$5,116	$4,115	$4,171	$6,846	$8,618	$8,973	$5,195
Money Spent	Jan	Feb	Mar	Apr	May	Jun	Jul	Aug	Sep	Oct	Nov	Dec
Cash Spending	$8,000	$8,000	$8,000	$8,000	$8,000	$8,000	$8,000	$8,000	$8,000	$8,000	$8,000	$8,000
Bill Payment	$12,000	$5,633	$6,957	$6,977	$6,018	$7,063	$5,971	$5,742	$5,736	$7,000	$8,150	$7,411
Repay Loans	$123	$26	$30	$134	$138	$142	$146	$151	$155	$160	$165	$170
Purchase Assets	$0	$0	$0	$0	$0	$0	$0	$0	$0	$0	$0	$0
Total Spent	$20,123	$13,759	$15,087	$15,111	$14,156	$15,205	$14,117	$13,893	$13,892	$15,160	$16,315	$15,581
Cash Flow	-$10,525	-$634	-$450	$610	$1,887	-$89	-$2	$278	$2,955	$3,458	$2,658	-$386
Cash Balance	-$10,525	$1,159	-$1,609	-$10,999	-$9,112	-$9,201	-$9,203	-$8,926	-$5,971	-$2,518	$45	-$241

Illustration A-3: Exploring Startup Cash Needs

That low point comes, theoretically, in the third month of the business, March. The low point is $11,609. Obviously that's just an educated guess, but it's based on assumptions for sales forecast, expense budget, and important cash flow factors including sales on account and purchasing inventory. So it's better than a stab in the dark, or some rule of thumb. Just as an example, the total spending with the estimates shown here, the theoretical "year's worth of spending," is $182,000 (which you don't see on the illustration, by the way, but take my word for it). The total for the first six months is $93,000. If Magda sticks to those old formulas, she can't start the business. She is able to raise enough money, between loans and her savings, to put $12,000 into the starting cash balance. So that's what she does. Then she launches and continues to have her monthly reviews, and watch the performance of all key indicators very carefully.

Find Your Startup Costs Sweet Spot

There is no magic startup costs estimate for a given business. Every startup has its own natural level of startup costs. It's built into the circumstances, like strategy, location, and resources. Call it the natural startup level; or maybe the sweet spot.

1. The Plan

For example, in the illustrations above, Magda's restaurant deli in the office park needs about $60,000, and Garrett's bicycle store needs about $125,000. The level is determined by factors like strategy, scope, founders' objectives, location, and so forth. In both cases, the entrepreneurs have lists of assets they need and expenses they'll incur. Let's call these lists the natural startup level, which is built into the nature of the business, something like DNA.

Startup cost estimates have three parts: a list of expenses, a list of assets needed, and an initial cash number calculated to cover the company through the early months when most startups are still too young to generate sufficient revenue to cover their monthly costs.

It's not just a matter of industry type or best practices; strategy, resources, and location make huge differences. The fact that it's a Vietnamese restaurant or a graphic arts business or a retail shoe store doesn't determine the natural startup level, by itself. A lot depends on where, by whom, with what strategy, and what resources.

While we don't know it for sure ever — because even after we count the actual costs, we can always second-guess our actual spending — I do believe we can understand something like natural levels, related to the nature of the specific startup.

Marketing strategy, for example, might make a huge difference. The company planning to buy web traffic will naturally spend much more in its early months than the company planning to depend on viral word of mouth. It's in the plan.

So too with location, product development strategy, management team and compensation, lots of different factors. They're all in the plan. They result in our natural startup level.

2. Funding or Not Funding

There's an obvious relationship between the amount of money needed and whether or not there's funding, and where and how you seek that funding. It's not random, it's related to the plan itself. Here again is the idea of a natural level, of a fit between the nature of the business startup, and its funding strategy.

It seems that you start with your own resources, and if that's enough, you stop

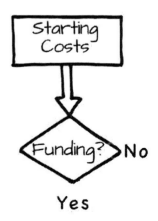

there too. You look at what you can borrow. And you deal with realities of friends and family (limited for most people), angel investment (for more money, but also limited by realities of investor needs, payoffs, etc.), and venture capital (available for only a few very high-end plans, with good teams, defensible markets, scalability, etc.).

3. Launch or Revise

Somewhere in this process is a sense of scale and reality. If the natural startup cost is $2 million but you don't have a proven team and a strong plan, then you don't just raise less money, and you don't just make do with less. No — and this is important — at that point, you have to revise your plan. You don't just go blindly on spending money (and probably dumping it down the drain) if the money raised, or the money you can raise, doesn't match the amount the plan requires.

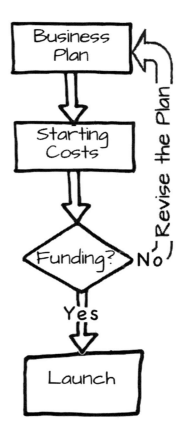

Revise the plan. Lower your sites. Narrow your market. Slow your projected growth rate.

Bring in a stronger team. New partners? More experienced people? Maybe a different ownership structure will help.

And don't forget what we call bootstrapping, which means launching a business without any outside investment. Scale it down to just what you can actually do without other people's money. I've done that myself and had it work to build a company that ended up profitable, with multi-million-dollar sales, no debt, and more than 50 employees. And when you do it without investors, you own it all yourself.

What's really important is you have to jump out of a flawed assumption set and revise the plan. I've seen this too often: people do the plan, set the amounts, fail the funding, and then just keep going, but without the needed funding.

And that's just not likely to work. More important, it is likely to cause you to fail and lose money. You need to revise the plan to fit the resources.

Repetition for emphasis: you revise the plan to give it a different natural need level. You don't just make do with less. You also do less. Otherwise, it's not realistic.

Appendix B

Sharing Your Plan

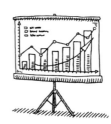

What do you do with your lean plan when you need to show it to outsiders? You dress it up. You take your core updated lean plan and add the summaries, descriptions, and supporting information you need to serve your business purpose.

This appendix explains how to take your lean plan and dress it up with a pitch presentation, summary memo, or elevator speech.

The Business Plan Event

I refer to the phrase "business plan event" as some business development that requires you to show a business plan to somebody. The most common business plan events relate to getting investments or business loans. Both of these business events require presenting a business plan to somebody outside your company. Other less obvious business plan events are triggered by divorce, death, opening a merchant account, bringing in partners, selling the business, and so forth.

Assess Your Specific Needs

Make sure you understand the real need for your specific business plan event. Always know who will read your plan and what they'll be looking for when they do. For example:

- Investors review a summary memo or executive summary, not the whole plan. If they like the summary, then they'll look for a short pitch. If they like the pitch, then they'll want a full plan to use for due diligence – and sometimes the lean plan is enough for due diligence purposes, without the elaborate plan. Always keep the summary, pitch, and latest lean business plan aligned so they all say the same thing, but for a different medium.

- Bankers want to see the company legal details and serious past financial results, along with a fairly standard description of the business, product, market, and team. They'll also want to see personal financial statements of business owners. And they like a good executive summary so they don't have to read the whole plan, just leaf through it to find the financials. So your lean plan plus a short summary may be enough because the formal loan application includes a lot of the details.

- Academics are the most likely to want to see a more traditional business plan with detailed market and industry analysis and sophisticated financial analysis such as NPV (net present value) and IRR (internal rate of return). I won't define either of these here because if you're in the academic mode you have plenty of information on that already; and if you aren't, you don't need them. Real investors and bankers pay no attention to either of these analyses.

These are just a few examples. There are also plans related to new expansions inside larger companies, divorce settlements, retirement and estate planning, selling a business, valuation for tax purposes, and other business plan events.

Tip: "Business plan" means different things to different people. If you're not sure what's required for a specific business plan event, ask. Ask a person who will be reading the plan. Ask for a sample of one she or he likes. Ask what format, how long, what it should cover. You shouldn't have to guess.

Lead with Stories

"All human beings have an innate need to hear and tell stories and to have a story to live by."

– Harvey Cox

Before you write, before you do summaries or slides, get your stories straight. The stories apply to all the variations of communications with outsiders, plan, pitch, or whatever.

Every year I see several dozen business pitches, I read hundreds of summary memos, and I read 50 or more formal business plans. The best of them lead with stories. For example, they start by presenting a problem and follow with their business' solution to that problem. Some start with a market story, highlighting the need. There is no magic formula defining which story to use, exactly; but the plan for outsiders is to describe and explain, so stories are essential. Numbers are nice too, but stories give the numbers context and relevance.

Start with an image that illustrates the problem. A plan for a new high-tech smog-free technology starts with a picture of a smog-choked city. A pitch for distributing restaurant leftovers to homeless people starts with a picture of the garbage area behind a restaurant, full of discarded food. A pitch for a worldwide crafts market starts with a picture of an African woman who would be able to sell her crafts worldwide using just her mobile phone.

When you can't illustrate a more abstract problem, highlight a person or people who have a need and will benefit from the solution. A plan for a video game that helps autistic children starts with a close-up of a specific child and his parents. A pitch for a new medical technology starts with two  aging baby boomers. I still remember one that started with a graveyard and a claim for a percent of deaths that could be reduced by a new device.

Make it dramatic. You want to inspire as well as communicate. You want your audience to see it for themselves, in their own imaginations.

And maintain the drama with the solution. In the first example above, they showed a picture of their new-technology clean-air brick ovens installed and working. In the second, they showed a branded delivery vehicle outside a homeless shelter. In the third, it was a picture of a rudimentary mobile phone with programming on it superimposed over one of the major crafts online sites.

Be strategic, and sensitive to your unique story. Depending on what works, you might use a picture of the product, or the website, maybe the technology team, or whatever works to highlight what you want to show to your specific business audience.

The stories with pictures are especially important with the business pitches, which are normally slide decks done in PowerPoint or Keynote; but it also works with business plan documents and summary memos. Even a 60-second elevator speech works better going from problem to solution to how this company is uniquely positioned to develop and sell that solution.

Develop Summaries

I would have written a shorter letter,
but I did not have the time.

– Blaise Pascal

Keep your summary short, cover the highlights, and assume key people will read this summary and nothing else. It's a front door. Whether it's an executive summary that comes first in a document, or a summary memo, make that reader want more information.

A good summary is a collection of tips of the iceberg. Each one has enough information to imply its entire iceberg, but it can't go too deep, and it has to leave the iceberg somewhere. Don't promise in the summary anything you can't back up in the document or following discussions.

As your plan changes, rewrite and revise your summary to keep it fresh and keep it aligned with the plan.

What to Include in the Summary

As you summarize, keep in mind the nature of your business plan event. Choose what to include based on specific needs.

Different experts have different opinions on the ideal length of a summary. I've always recommended a summary of 2-5 pages, which can be used as a stand-alone summary memo where that's appropriate. For example, in my angel investment group, we don't read full business plans of all the startups that apply for investment. We eliminate some proposals from just reading the summary. We read the full business plans only after deciding, from the summary, that we want to know more.

A generalized summary will include the obvious information such as essential business details, what you sell, what locations, projected sales growth, profitability, and news you don't want anybody to miss. It's a good place to put a highlights chart, a bar chart that shows sales, gross margin, and profits before interest and taxes for the next three years. You should also cite and explain those numbers in the text.

However, generalized summaries are as rare as generalized business plan events. Write a new summary for each new event. Tailor it to match the requirements of your specific business plan event.

For example, a plan to be used while seeking investment performs a sales function. You are selling your concept, your startup, or your growing company to an outsider who is interested in becoming an investor. So put yourself in the investor's place and emphasize the elements that will make her money. Put management team, market potential, scalability, defensibility, and possible exits where she can see them.

Highlight whatever is strongest about your plan, compared to others. So if you have a venture already backed by major brand-name backers, say so early in the summary. If you've got a founders team that includes several known entrepreneurs with good track records, then put it up front. If you have a good business track record, like impressive early sales or landmark deals with major channels, corporations or governments, put that first. If you have an amazing new invention or break-through technology, lead with that. Use good judgment. You're an editor, at this point, looking at things through the audience's eyes.

Summary Formats

- An executive summary can be the first chapter of a business plan document or a stand-alone document separate from the business plan. It assumes the more elaborate document exists. It can be printed, sent as an electronic (PDF) document, or left on the web with password protection.

- A summary memo stands alone. It can be a document on its own or attached to an email, or it can be text in an email.

- You may also need to summarize a market analysis, competition, marketing plan, or product plan as an addition to a lean business plan when facing some business plan events. These, however, often appear in pitches instead of as summary documents.

- What people refer to as a one-page business plan is also a summary. Occasionally a one-page summary is called a pitch, or a business pitch.

- I've seen short videos serve as summaries. They have to be just a few minutes, ideally just one minute, never more than three. They cover the same ground as the summary. They are usually password protected.

- An elevator speech is also a summary, but delivered quickly – in as little as a single minute – and verbally.

Your Business Pitch

> *"The purpose of a pitch is to stimulate interest,*
> *not to close a deal."*
>
> – Guy Kawasaki

A business pitch is a presentation. It includes a deck of slides that serves as a presentation aid and background, and the verbal discussion that begins as a planned talk and ends up with questions and answers. The classic pitch is one delivered by startup founders to potential investors. That same pitch is also used in business classrooms and business plan and venture competitions, in which students and startup founders pitch to judges, who are usually investors.

There are two kinds of slide decks associated with the business pitch. The first and most important is the deck intended for the presentation itself. That's the one you read about most often. It should be almost entirely images, each slide with its title and an image, but very little text. The images are photographs, business charts, and diagrams. It keeps the focus of attention on the speaker, not the slides. It doesn't encourage the audience to read text from the slides. It doesn't have bullet points people will read.

The second kind of pitch deck should be called the leave-behind pitch. It stands alone, to be read, not presented. It should reflect the main presentation and cover the same content. It might even have the same number of slides in the same order as the main presentation; but it has a lot more words because its business purpose requires that.

Don't confuse the two: A pitch to be read must be very different from a pitch that supports a live presentation with you talking. These require different styles for different business situations.

Most of what you read about business pitches focuses on the pitch deck and pitch presentation startup founders deliver to potential investors.

In either case, what you want to show is something like this (but be flexible and sensitive to your specific audience and specific business situation; this is just a sample):

- Problem: Show a problem to solve, ideally one that investors will understand immediately, and relate to. You can refer to examples in the previous section, Lead With Stories.

- Solution: How is your startup going to solve that problem? What do you do? Ideally, the solution is something investors will also understand and relate to. And there is a good image to show. You can refer to examples of this one also in Lead With Stories.

- Market potential: How many people/buyers have the problem and how much is the solution worth? If the story works, the numbers are supplemental, but good to show. If the story doesn't work, nobody cares about the numbers.

- Secret sauce: You decide what to highlight here, depending on the audience. Investors and business plan contest judges want to see technology, trade secrets, existing market position, or some other fact that helps you establish barriers to entry and protect your competitive advantage.

- The team: Investors need to see a credible startup team, with previous startup experience and background and experience specifically related to the problem and the opportunity.

- Traction: Show milestones achieved, momentum, traffic, anything you can to make your story – and the opportunity – presentable. Web traffic or downloads are excellent. Success on Kickstarter is also excellent. Early sales, and firm commitments from important clients or distributors are also good.

- All the rest: Flesh it out as needed, depending on your specific case, with highlights investors will look for. Exit strategies, competition, market strategy. Be sure to have projected P&L as a bar chart and have solid projected P&L, Balance, and Cash Flow to back it up.

Now go find David S. Rose's TED talk on pitching for investors, and find some of Nancy Duarte's work on storytelling and presentations – her TED talks or her book *Resonate*, and look up on the web Guy Kawasaki content for "The Art of the Pitch," a chapter in his book *The Art of the Start*. You might also do a web search for Seth Godin's *Death by PowerPoint*.

Your Elevator Speech

> *"The only people who don't need*
> *elevator pitches are elevator salesmen."*
>
> – Jarod Kinz

If you can't say it in 60 seconds, you have a problem. Your strategy isn't clear enough. Nowadays we call it "the elevator speech," meaning a quick description of the business that you could do in the time you share with a stranger in an elevator. It's becoming popular in the everyday language of the entrepreneur, venture capitalist, and the teaching of entrepreneurship.

I don't think it's academic. I think it's important. I think it's a great exercise that everybody in business should be able to do. Let's get simple, let's get focused, and let's get powerful.

Your lean plan is simple and concise. What better way to condense it than in a quick elevator speech? If you can't do it, worry.

Part 1: Personalize

As I said in Lead with Stories, start with a problem, and use a good example to make it stand out. Start your speech with a person (or business, or organization) in a situation. Personalize. Identify clearly. For example:

Terry is a successful business owner worried about social media. She knows her business should be on Twitter, Facebook, and the other major platforms, but she's already busy running a business, and she doesn't have time to do meaningful social media as well (Have Presence).

Jane Smith wants to do her own business plan. She knows her business and what she wants to do, but needs help organizing the plan and getting the right pieces together. The plan needs to look professional because she's promised to show it to her bank as part of the merchant account process (LivePlan).

Notice that in both of these examples I could be much more general. Have Presence targets small business owners. Business Plan Software is for the do-it-yourselfer who wants good business planning. But instead of generally describing a market, I've made it personal. Details and granularity work.

Sometimes you can get away with generalizing. "Farmers in the Willamette Valley," for example, or "parents of gifted children." It's an easy way to slide into describing a market. However, I suspect that you're almost always better off starting with a more readily imaginable single person, and let that person stand for your target market.

Part 2: Why You

In the next part of your elevator speech address "why you"? Why your business? What's special about you that makes your offering or solution interesting to the target person or organization you just identified?

This is where you bring in your background, your core competence, your track record, your management team, or whatever. For example:

Have Presence is a small business like her own, run by three co-owners who love social media, understand small business, and do only thoughtful, strategic social media updates for clients they know and represent well.

Palo Alto Software has dedicated itself to business planning for more than 20 years. Its founder is one of the best-known experts in the field. Its current management team grew up with business planning, in the trenches. The 8-person development team has more than 50 person years in the same focused area.

What we focus on here is core competence and differentiation. And, in the classic elevator speech, you have to say it fast. You make your point quickly and go on.

Make sure your point is the right point: benefits to the target customer. It's not what's great about you, but rather, what about you lends credibility to your ability to meet the need and solve the problem.

I've included two different paragraphs for the same company on purpose. See how the unique qualifications differ for different contexts. The descriptions have to change for each.

You might also think of this as the classic "What do you bring to the party?" question. It's not just your brilliance or good looks or great track record, it's fostering credibility for solving the problem.

Part 3: What You Offer

Now explain what that potential buyer (or investor) gets. Or the organization. You've personalized the need or want, identified your unique qualities to solve the problem, and now you have to put the need or want in concrete terms that anybody can see. For example:

The Have Presence staff gives Terry thoughtful, strategic social media updates for clients they know and represent well. They don't tell Terry what and how to do it. Instead, they do the work, manage the social media, and give her business social media presence, for a monthly fee that's considerably less than a half-time employee, without the long-term commitment.

LivePlan lets Jane jump into and out of her business plan at a moment's notice whenever she wants. She can start with the core strategy and build it in blocks, planning while she goes, refining projections as needed. It's built around a solid error-checked, financially and mathematically correct financial model, and a generalized set of suggestions for outlines, but is also completely flexible for adding and deleting topics and creating a unique business plan. Each task, whether topic or table, comes with easy-to-understand instructions and useful examples.

In each example here we see clearly how this meets the need or solves the problem. Forget features as much as possible, and illustrate benefits. You've already described the person with the situation, and built up your ability to solve it, so now it's just about the solution. Stay focused and concentrated. People will get one or at the most two unique attributes of your business offering. Don't confuse them with more.

Part 4: Close Well. Ask for What You Need

The close depends on who you are and what you want. If you've personalized in the first part, sold yourself and/or your organization in the second, and established the attractiveness or suitability of the business offering in the third, it's time to finish strong with a closing.

Your closing depends completely on context. What do you want from the person or people you're talking to? The classic elevator speech context is for a venture competition or a search for investors. But there's also the true elevator speech for the established company, simply describing your company to somebody who asked, with no real close. Be honest, you're not always asking for an order, even when you're just chatting with the person in the next seat on the airplane. If you are trying to sell then do ask for the order. Seriously: "if you give me a card, I'll send you a copy with an invoice." Seriously: ask for the order. "If you don't like it, send it back. Here's my card."

For the venture competition or investment variety elevator speech, don't try to convey too much information. Do establish in general terms where you are or what you want. "We're looking for seed money of half a million dollars." Or "We're now raising round-two financing of three million dollars to be used for the mainstream marketing launch." Or "We're looking for serious marketing partners able to put money up front in return for privileged first-year pricing." Or "We're trying to establish a royalty relationship with an appropriate manufacturer." And then, ask for a business card, and give one. "If you know anybody who might fit that bill, feel free to recommend us." Or "Please give me a call." Don't offer to send a business plan, and don't ask directly when it's about investment; reduce the awkwardness by suggesting that your audience might know somebody, not that your audience might invest.

Don't talk terms in the elevator speech. Just establish what you want or need.

If you're in a real elevator with a real potential investor, you probably soft pedal: "If you know anybody who might be interested, please pass this along. Or maybe you want a business card and permission to send a follow-up email."

And if you're doing an elevator speech in a business venture competition — close with an appropriate call for investment. Venture competitions are always keying on the would-be or hypothetical pitch to the investor, so make it clear. The better ones end up with something relatively definitive like a reference to seed capital or first-round equity investment. Stay general. Make them want more.

Appendix C

Planning for Angel Investment

"The more angels we have in Silicon Valley, the better. We are funding innovation. We are funding the next Facebook, Google, and Twitter."

— Ron Conway, well-known Silicon Valley angel investor

Angel investment? Allow me to help you understand what that is, whether or not it applies to you, how it works, and how your lean business plan fits into the process. And this is about *investment*, not a loan, and not a grant. Somebody invests in your business by giving the business money to spend. In return, the investor buys a share of your business. You don't pay the investor back, as you would for a loan. The investors get a return on investment if and when they can sell the share of your business they bought for a profit. For example, angel investors buy 40% of your company for $400,000, and then they sell that share three years later for $1.2 million. The return on the initial investment was 200% (800/400). We can calculate from these numbers that the valuation of the company for the initial investment was $1 million, and at *exit* (when the investor sells out), it was $3 million (40%/$1.2M).

Sometimes a person buys a share in a business in order to contribute to the business, help run it, take a salary perhaps, or share in the profits, but not necessarily to sell the ownership in a few years. That's not angel investment. And when your rich aunt gives you $25,000 to start a business, that's friends and family investment if she then owns a share of your company; and generosity and family spirit if she doesn't.

You don't pay investors back. You make your business worth more so they can sell their shares to somebody else to get a return, at exit.

There are books for angel investors, books about angel investors, and books about how to secure angel investment. There are also several well-known angel investment platforms. The website at gust.com is a platform for angel investors and entrepreneurs to share information, and it has a wealth of information about angels, in videos and articles. The Angel Capital Association (http://www.angelcapitalassociation.org/) has directories, definitions, lists, and explanations. You can also check out AngelList and do a web search for "angel investors."

Angel investors generally focus on seed money – early investment for startups at early stages of growth – for amounts less than $1 million. Several experts have different definitions of angel investment, on how many angel investors exist, and how much money they invest. As I write this in 2015, the latest available statistics (Illustration C-1) come from 2013. Approximately 300,000 angel investors did 71,000 deals with startups, mostly for seed financing and early stages.

US Angel Investors in 2013	US Venture Capital in 2013
$24.8 billion	$29.6 billion
71,000 deals	4,050 deals
32,000 seed	120 seed
29,000 early stage	1,375 early stage
9,200 expansion	2,550 later/expansion
300,000 individuals	548 active firms

source: Angel Capital Association, Center for Venture Research/UNH, NVCA 2014 Yearbook; PwC Money Tree

Illustration C-1: Angel Investment and Venture Capital

Legally, Angel investment is people who are accredited investors as defined by the U.S. Securities and Exchange Commission (SEC), which sets wealth criteria:

- *Either earned income that exceeded $200,000 (or $300,000 together with a spouse) in each of the prior two years, and reasonably expects the same for the current year;*

- *or has a net worth over $1 million, either alone or together with a spouse (excluding the value of the person's primary residence).*

Those rules were going to relax with the Jobs Act of 2012, which was supposed to open the gate to crowdfunding, but hasn't yet (see below, on crowdfunding). Startups looking for investment are still going to angel investors pretty much the same way they have for several decades. And angel investors are still mostly wealthy individuals, often with tech industry background, often former entrepreneurs whose former endeavors succeeded. There are listings of angel investors on the web, and gust.com lists more than 600 groups of angel investors operating in the United States and elsewhere.

Outside Investors

First, I see this confusion a lot: People use the terms *venture capital*, *venture capitalist*, and *VC* to apply to any outsider investing in a startup. However, it's useful to draw some distinctions in this area, between three important classifications: venture capital, angel investors, and anybody else.

Venture Capital

Venture capital means big-money investment managed by professional investors spending other people's money. The money comes from extremely wealthy people, insurance companies, university endowments, big corporations, etc. Think of Kleinert Perkins et al., First Round, Softbank, Oak, etc. Venture capital usually comes in millions of dollars. Over the last few years, Venture Capital has moved towards larger investments for companies further along the business growth cycle, and away from smaller investments for true startups.

The most important distinctions between angels and VCS are:

- Angels invest their own money; VCs invest other people's money.

- Angel investment is much more likely to be in hundreds of thousands than in millions of dollars.

- Aside from those two distinctions, it is generally true that VCs will be more rigorous in studying (called "due diligence") the investment before they make it. Both angels and VCs will have similar processes for looking at summaries, then pitches, then business plans.

Friends and Family

Anything else is called "friends and family," which really means "not VC" and "not angel investment." The laws on investment allow a few so-called friends and family, but there are limits. The intention of all the regulation in this area is to prevent the kind of stock frauds that were rampant during the Great Depression.

Will Your Business get Angel Investment?

Angel investment is an option for a small minority of startups that combine the right factors. There are always exceptions to the rule, but in general, to be interesting to angel investors, a business has to have at least these four qualities:

1. You need to show attractive potential growth in sales. Think of big growth, like from zero to $5 million annually, or even better, $10 or $20 million annually, in three to five years. Nobody can predict the future, but angel investors pride themselves on being able to make good guesses. From the entrepreneur's side of the table, that means having a credible growth story. Numbers aren't enough. Anybody can type numbers into a spreadsheet. You need a story, along the lines I included earlier in Lead with Stories. Angel investors will read your story and build their own guess about the company's potential. At that point, the numbers (market analysis, demographics, research) are useful if the story rings true.

2. You need to be able to grow with scale. That means your business can increase its unit sales very fast without having a proportionate increase in fixed costs, head count and marketing expenses. Most product businesses can scale larger by adding capacity to a product manufacturing process in a relatively easy fashion. Most web businesses can grow easily since it's relatively simple to add proper bandwidth when increasing the number of users of a website or application. But service businesses often suffer the problem of

needing to increase personnel to grow. Investors call it a *body shop* when doubling sales is possible only by doubling the fixed costs and numbers of employees; and that's not a good thing. Sometimes service businesses will try to generate scale with franchising. But franchising isn't a credible option for angel investors until you have a very successful working first venue (or two or three).

3. You need to have some way to ward off or delay competition. Investors talk about a so-called *secret sauce*, or technology, patents, trade secret, or some way to create barriers to entry. The worry is that a well-funded big company will jump in on a new business, outspend it and take away its opportunity. People talk of the so-called *first mover advantage* that makes an idea defensible if the initial entrant to the market grows fast and builds its customer base very quickly. That works sometimes, but not always. Investors will use their own judgment in reviewing the idea, not necessarily what you tell them.

4. You need a credible management team. Angel investors are not likely to invest in a startup that doesn't have at least one founder who has already been involved in a startup. This is disappointing to first-time entrepreneurs, but the fact is that in startups, nothing substitutes for experience.

The Normal Process for Angel Investment

First of all, there is no normal. Angel investors are individuals, investing their own money. Many join groups that will invite startups to pitch for the group; but many operate as individuals. So what I say here is what's common, what I'm familiar with, and what usually happens.

It starts with an introduction. The easiest version of the introduction is a formal submission to an angel investment group, using one of the angel platforms like gust.com or Angel List (angellist.co). Also, you can ask for an introduction from somebody you know who might know angel investors: maybe a business school professor, or somebody from a local chamber of commerce. Or perhaps you attend a business event. Angel investors don't normally read unsolicited emails, but there are exceptions to every rule. If you're talking to a potential angel investor, keep your <u>elevator speech</u> (Appendix B) in mind, and if the occasion fits, use it.

The angel investors will look at your <u>summaries</u> – a summary memo sent via email, perhaps, or a business summary submitted on one of the platforms. This is in Appendix B.

If the summary catches their attention, and they like what they see there, you'll be invited to do a <u>business pitch</u>. This is also in Appendix B.

If they hear the pitch, ask questions, get some answers, and are still interested, then they'll want to see your business plan. That used to be the standard formal business plan, what the lean startup people call the elaborate business plan. However, times are changing, and almost all angel investors will settle for just the lean business plan after they've met you, talked with you, and heard your business pitch. Your lean plan, summary memo, pitch deck, and perhaps some additional details on your market and traction is enough for the due diligence every conscientious investor does before making the investment.

Due diligence is a serious process that takes weeks at least, and often months. Investors need to check lots of details including legal specifics, contracts, deals with suppliers and distributors, important customers, technology, patents, and other things. It's extremely rare to go from introduction to depositing a check in a matter of weeks.

Appendix D

Lean Plan with LivePlan

"LivePlan has reinvented business planning. It's the only tool that helps entrepreneurs track their progress with a unique dashboard specifically designed for small business."

—John Jantsch

This is the first mention in this book of LivePlan, on the web at **www.liveplan.com, a business planning web app available on a subscription basis, published by Palo Alto Software.** I'm the founder and majority owner of the company. LivePlan was developed by a team of professionals who respected my views on business planning. It keeps getting better, so by the time you read this it may have more specific adaptations for the lean business plan. As of now, it is already completely compatible.

However, to avoid confusion, please let me clarify: *Nothing in this book requires LivePlan.* Lean business planning isn't a matter of software, word processing, spreadsheet, or any other tools. This appendix is here simply as a convenience to readers who might already be working with LivePlan. Furthermore, there is a version of this book that is written specifically for LivePlan users, which is available to you absolutely free if you own this one, so if that's the case, just go to the website at leanplan.com and use the contact page to ask.

Here are some specifics related to this book:

1. In general, the LivePlan outline is more than you need. Do just a lean plan, not everything the default outline suggests. Feel free to ignore any topics.

2. Don't write finished text, but just bullets. Don't do anything you don't need.

3. For strategy, just use the LivePlan pitch. That's enough. And if you want more, add a topic into the Strategy and Implementation chapter. Call it Strategy. Keep it short, just bullets.

4. For tactics use the default Marketing Plan topic in the and create a list of Strategy and Implementation section but just use bullet points and list sales-and-marketing-related topics. Use the Product and Services topic in the Product and Services section to list tactics related to your business offering. Use the default Management Team topic in the Company section for any other tactics.

5. For concrete specifics, the Schedule tab on the top is great for review schedules and milestones. Try to add the performance metrics right into the Milestones descriptions in the Schedule. Add a topic anywhere you like in the LivePlan outline for assumptions.

6. LivePlan is a great tool for essential business numbers. Make sure you go to settings to specify more detail. Then use the Forecast tab to do the:

   - Sales Forecast (LivePlan calls that Revenue Forecast at this writing, but it is going to change to Sales);
   - Personnel Plan;
   - Budget (that's spending budget, because it includes spending and buying assets);
   - Cash Flow Assumptions;
   - And Loans and Investments.

LivePlan Does Formal Financial Projections

When you're done you also have excellent cash flow projections and formal financial projections, both mathematically correct and financially correct, in the format most banks and analysts want them. Those are in LivePlan as Projected Profit and Loss Statement, Projected Balance Sheet, and Projected Cash Flow Statement.

LivePlan is Excellent for Ongoing Management

The LivePlan Scoreboard is ideal for planning as management. Connect it to your accounting software, and you'll have automatic plan vs. actual analysis, in a dashboard with flexible options for viewing different factors. It's great for those monthly management meetings.

CPSIA information can be obtained at www.ICGtesting.com
Printed in the USA
LVOW10s2109060616

491420LV00017B/1286/P